Gym and Tonic

A play

John Godber

Samuel French — London
New York - Toronto - Hollywood

GYM AND TONIC

First performed at the Derby Playhouse on 10th October 1996, with the following cast:

Don Weston	James Hornsby
Shirley Weston	Gilly Tompkins
Gertrude Tate	Marcia Warren
Ken Blake	William Ilkley
Zoë	Justine Glenton
Chloë	Justine Glenton
Maggie	Marcia Warren
Sam	James Weaver
Shaun	James Weaver
Bellboy	James Weaver

Directed by John Godber
Designed by Alison Taylor
Lighting by Alexandra Stafford

CHARACTERS

Don Weston, 39/40
Shirley Weston, 37
Gertrude Tate, 72
Ken Blake, 42
Zoë, 27
Chloë, 23
Maggie Weston, 65
Sam Weston, 13
Shaun, 21
Bellboy, 20

The parts of **Zoë** and **Chloë** can be doubled; **Maggie Weston** can be played by the actress playing **Gertrude Tate**; the parts of **Shaun**, the **Bellboy** and **Sam Weston** can be trebled.

The action takes place over a week at Scardale Hall Health Hydro somewhere in the heart of England

Time — the present

Other plays by John Godber published by
Samuel French Ltd

April in Paris
Blood Sweat and Tears
Happy Families
Lucky Sods
Passion Killers
Salt of the Earth
Teechers
Up 'n' Under
Up 'n' Under II
Weekend Breaks

ACT I
SCENE 1

Scardale Hall Health Hydro. Aerobics Studio

There is a raised area at the rear of the stage with three windows in the back wall; steps lead down to stage level on both sides. The walls and floor are of stone. There is a cupboard at the back of the DS area

As the CURTAIN *rises, the DS area is laid out as an aerobics studio, with equipment for a step class; sports bags belonging to the participants are scattered about*

Disco music plays from a portable cassette player on stage. The Lights slowly come up on a step class in progress

Zoë, the tutor, is taking a small group through a step session. Shirley, Ken, and Shaun all move to Zoë's commands. Zoë is extremely fit and puts the rest of the class through their paces. We watch for some time before the dialogue starts

Zoë And step! And swing those arms; and march, keep it moving, keep it nice and free, no tension. March. Shaun, good! Come on, Shirley, that's good. Ken, push it. And step, and swing and over we go, and turn, and biceps curl. Everybody say yo!
All Everybody say yo!

Don Weston enters. He is a mild-mannered businessman approaching forty. He is distinctly out of place. He goes to the back of the class and tries to join in with the session but is hopelessly out of step, despite trying very hard. Shirley, his wife, acknowledges him with some disdain

Zoë And one last time!

They repeat the sequence

And "spotty dog".

They all do the "spotty dog". The group follows Zoë's following instructions with varying degrees of success

That's good. Now bring it slowly to a halt, and come to rest. And shake out … And relax and breathe, good. Nice round of applause.

They all applaud themselves. Zoë turns off the music

Everybody say yo!
All (*breathlessly*) Everybody say yo.
Don Yo.
Zoë OK, that's good. That's great. OK, Shirley?
Shirley Just about.
Zoë You've done well.
Shirley I can't get my breath.
Zoë Just take it steady.
Shirley I've enjoyed it. I thought it would be a lot harder.
Zoë You OK, Shaun?
Shaun Well, I'm sweating, and I feel like a prat, but ——
Zoë That is the idea.
Shaun Right.
Zoë OK, Ken?
Ken Fine.
Zoë You'll have to come to the Reebok slide; that'll test you.
Ken Sounds good.
Zoë It will. I mean it!
Ken Is that a threat?
Zoë Could be.
Shaun Can I go now?
Zoë What have you got next?
Shaun Back and neck.
Zoë Great.
Shaun I should be asleep in no time.
Ken Hang on, I'll come with you — I just fancy a coffee. See you later. Nice to meet you. Maybe see you in the conservatory; you can stuff yourself in there.
Shirley Yes, that's more my thing.
Zoë See you in the gym?
Ken Is that a promise? (*To Don*) Bit late, mate?
Don Better late than never.

Shaun and Ken exit

Don moves from the back of the class and heads DS. *Zoë stacks the steps in the cupboard* US

Shirley (*to Zoë, about Ken*) He's full of it, isn't he?
Zoë Well, he's fit.
Shirley Unlike mine.
Don I heard that.
Shirley Took your time.
Don I couldn't find my trainers.
Shirley I wouldn't bother coming if that's all you're going to do.
Don I liked the "spotty dog" bit. I was waiting for the "Little Weed".
Zoë That's tomorrow.
Shirley That is Zoë, Don.
Zoë Hiya.
Don Hi.
Zoë Right, well, I'd better nip off. I'm on the pool next.
Shirley So you do that as well, then?
Zoë No rest for the wicked.
Shirley I'll probably not be able to walk tomorrow. It's the first time I've
    done anything physical for about two years.
Zoë You did really well.
Shirley Listen you don't have to be kind. I know I'm a bit overweight.
Zoë It's how you feel though, isn't it?
Shirley Yes, but I feel a bit overweight.
Zoë I worry about trying to put weight on.
Shirley (*to Zoë*) He missed me doing my thing, didn't he?
Zoë You'll have to come earlier next time.
Don I think more than five minutes might be a bit too much for my knees.
Shirley The most physical thing he does is run to the car.
Don Yeah, but we've got a long drive.
Shirley You should do this, it's brilliant.
Don I did do it.
Zoë What's wrong; don't you dance?
Don It's the Lycra, it scares me.
Zoë It's not compulsory.
Shirley He could dance. He played rugby and all sorts.
Don Years ago.
Zoë Oh, here we go! You're not old; I've got a judge in his sixties who works
    out here. How long have you been here?
Don About two hours. I've been waiting for my health check in the clinic.
Zoë Well, there's beginners' aerobics twice a day, a morning class and this
    one. Make sure you come to the slide; we'll get you sorted.

Zoë picks up her cassette player and her sports bag, and exits

Don She looks like the real thing.

Shirley Why were you late?
Don There was a queue at the treatment centre.
Shirley Oh right!
Don Somebody's leg had fallen off during a massage, I think.
Shirley I knew I'd end up doing it on my own. We never do anything together.
Don And I've been for a sniff about and all.
Shirley So have you booked for any treatments?
Don (*producing his daily itinerary; a short list*) One or two; and they took my blood pressure and I've had my metabolic rate checked. They wanted to find out how fit I am.
Shirley And how fit are you?
Don Not very, according to the nurse.
Shirley Well, you knew that.
Don That cost me thirty quid, I could have told them that for nothing. So what have you got next, then?
Shirley (*producing her itinerary*) I've got a Cellu M6 massage at three. Seaweed body wrap at four. A facial. A multi-method. My art class — I'm doing pottery — and there's a talk on stress relief.
Don Put me down for that.
Shirley And then there's T'ai Ch'i.
Don Is that for all week?
Shirley No that's just today. You've just got to learn to wind down! Zoë said, the only way you can get rid of stress is by exercise.
Don She didn't say anything about a bottle of Fleurie and a piece of brie, did she?
Shirley I've got to dash; I've got my Equilibrium.
Don What's that?
Shirley Neck and scalp massage.
Don Look at you.
Shirley Go to the lounge and chat to somebody.
Don You what, they're all that stuck up I'm frightened to open my mouth. They look at me like I've got a dick sticking out of the top of my head.
Shirley You have half the time.
Don I'm not wearing a dressing-gown.
Shirley Go and find that Ken; he seems like one of us.
Don What, poor?
Shirley We're not poor.
Don There's four Rolls-Royces parked outside, you know? A new Toyota looks a bit sick at the side of them, doesn't it? There was a woman in the reception who spoke so posh I thought she was a foreigner.
Shirley What's up? Do they scare you?
Don She did. We should've gone somewhere a bit more down-market.

Shirley Don't get so stressed out. What have you got next?
Don A massage.
Shirley Well, that should be good.
Don I don't fancy it, to be honest.
Shirley Why?
Don Well, it's a bit embarassing.
Shirley Why, have you got a spotty back again?
Don No, that's dried up.
Shirley It's just a back massage; what did you think it was?
Don Well, you never know your luck.
Shirley I don't think they do "extras".
Don I feel a bit shy about getting my kit off.
Shirley I had one when I came before, it's brilliant. They rub oils all over you, and you just drift. (*She grabs her things and makes to exit*)
Don Do you think I should ring to see if the kids are all right?
Shirley I've rung already.
Don And are they?
Shirley Holly's going out and Sam's on the internet.
Don How's Mum?
Shirley I didn't speak to her I spoke to Sam.
Don I'll give her a ring.
Shirley Why don't you leave it.
Don I'll ring her, see if she's OK.
Shirley Do what you want, then ... Look, I'm going to be late; it's not fair. (*She moves to exit again*)
Don So where do I go for the massage then?
Shirley To the treatments area. You know, I thought this would be your dream — surrounded by nubile young women?
Don It would have been, twenty years ago.
Shirley Twenty years ago you were surrounded by beautiful young women.
Don I feel like I'm somebody's stupid uncle now.
Shirley Well, spare us the card tricks.
Don Stupid uncles are forty, aren't they?
Shirley So are stupid dads.
Don Hey, you can go off people, you know?
Shirley I know that; I'm going off you already. (*She makes another attempt to depart*)

Don remains DS

Don Knowing my luck I'll probably have some hairy-arsed ex-marine doing my massage.
Shirley Sounds like just what I need — lucky you.

Don Yeah, lucky me.

Delightfully light classical music plays

  Shirley exits

Don remains on stage

The Lights change to a different setting on the DS area

A wicker chair is set up US

Don moves US and sits expectantly on the chair

SCENE 2
Treatment Room

Chloë, an attractive masseuse, enters pushing a massage table, with towels, bottles of oil etc.. She wears a pristine white coat which is decked out with various product badges. She brings the table to an abrupt halt DS and walks towards Don

The music fades

Chloë Mr Preston?
Don Weston.
Chloë Sorry?
Don Don Weston.
Chloë Sorry.
Don It's OK, I feel like I'm someone else.
Chloë Back and neck?
Don And two arms and legs.
Chloë Back and neck massage?
Don (*producing his itinerary*)That's what it says here.
Chloë I'm Chloë.
Don I'm Don.
Chloë I thought it was Preston. Sorry. Back and neck?
Don I think so.
Chloë Right. Have you ever had a massage before?
Don No.
Chloë Right.
Don Well, actually I had one years ago.
Chloë At Scardale Hall?

Don No, at university.
Chloë Oh, right. Was it good?
Don From what I can remember of it.
Chloë Was it a full body?
Don No, it was after a lot of coffee and a chat about Kafka.
Chloë I don't think we do that one.
Don I'm not surprised. Neither of us were sure when to make the move, so I just sat there and massaged this girl for five hours.
Chloë That sounds nice.
Don She fell asleep and I went back to do my thesis.
Chloë Oh dear.
Don It was probably the longest massage in the history of the world. My hands were bleeding at the end.
Chloë Five hours is a long time. So you haven't been to Scardale before?
Don No. My wife has. She came for a day two years ago. She loves it.
Chloë Well, lovely, I hope you have a wonderful stay.
Don Fingers crossed.
Chloë Well, if you'd just like to get comfortable.
Don Sorry?
Chloë Would you like to undress?
Don Oh, right.
Chloë Please.
Don Just here?
Chloë Please. I'll get the oils ready.
Don What shall I do then, just strip off?
Chloë Please.
Don Right.
Chloë And then get on the table.
Don Right.
Chloë Yeah.
Don Strip off, and then on the table.
Chloë Face down.
Don Face down?
Chloë Face down on the table please.
Don Right, strip off and then face down on the table.
Chloë I'm going to be using a blend of oils.
Don Erm ... Can I ...?
Chloë Yeah?
Don Do you mind if I leave my underpants on?
Chloë Well, we ——
Don I'm just a bit ...
Chloë We do normally expect you to ——
Don Oh, right.

Chloë — but if you'd rather take them off?
Don No, oh no.
Chloë Did you take your underpants off last time?
Don I think I probably did, to be honest. But it's sort of lost in the mists of time.
Chloë I think it would be better for both of us if you left them on.
Don I think you're right.
Chloë Just relax, you'll be fine. It doesn't hurt, you know.
Don No, I know. My wife and I used to massage each other but the most I get now is a pat on the head.
Chloë That's nice.
Don We don't need a dog.

Don strips down to his underpants during the following

Chloë Are you at the Hall for any particular reason?
Don Just to relax, really.
Chloë Oh, that'll be nice.
Don I'm forty on Thursday.
Chloë Oh good.
Don You're supposed to say, "You don't look it".
Chloë Sorry?
Don It's OK.
Chloë Isn't that funny, my uncle's forty this weekend.
Don Is he stupid?
Chloë Sorry?
Don Is he going a bit mad?
Chloë He is a bit wacky, now you come to mention it. Don't they say, life begins at forty?
Don I hope to God they're right. (*He reveals a very old-fashioned pair of underpants*) Sorry about this, you probably feel sick don't you?
Chloë No.
Don And you wouldn't say so if you did.
Chloë Exactly.
Don Yeah, forty at the weekend. I'm beginning to wonder how long I've got left.
Chloë Would you like to get on the table?
Don Yes, I think I should be able to manage that. (*He crawls on to the table and lays on his back*)
Chloë Other way, please.
Don Sorry. Face down.
Chloë Thanks.
Don I'm beginning to wonder if I'll ever see my kids grow up. I'm beginning to wonder if I'll ever see myself grow up to be honest.

Chloë How many do you have?
Don Selves?
Chloë Kids.
Don Two. Sam and Holly. I've got half a dozen selves.
Chloë I'm going to be using some deep relaxing oils. This should give you an all over warm sensation and give you a feeling of well-being.
Don I need that.
Chloë Well, when you've had a few days here you'll be completely sorted.
Don Yeah?
Chloë You'll just be able to let your mind wander.
Don Oh, no.
Chloë Why not?
Don I hate doing that. I hate it when it's all peaceful; my mind's overactive. I start to think about all sorts of morbid things.
Chloë Like what?
Don Death really.
Chloë Oh dear.
Don Yeah, my thoughts entirely. I've got to be working all the time; whenever I start to relax I start asking the big questions.
Chloë And what are the big questions?
Don Why?
Chloë Why what?
Don Why everything? When I was three we were playing in the soil after it had been raining and apparently I asked my Dad, "Why is mud?" I've been asking questions ever since.

Chloë puts oil on Don's back

Chloë This might seem a little bit ——
Don (*reacting*) Arhhh.
Chloë —— cold.
Don Ooohh.
Chloë There you go.
Don So how long have you been here, then?

Chloë slowly massages Don during the following; she is not too rough, just firm. He can hardly speak

Chloë Ten months. I trained at Champney's before I came here.
Don Is this it for you then, massaging backs for the rest of your life?
Chloë I fancy doing a cruise really.
Don Sounds nice.
Chloë Is that good?
Don Mmmmmm.

Chloë I think I'll stay here for another six months and then try and get on a cruise ship.

Don Mmmmmm.

Chloë This is very tight.

Don Mmmmmm.

Chloë Good.

Don Mmmmmm.

Chloë You're quite tense around the shoulders.

Don Mmmmmm.

Chloë Your back's quite bumpy.

Don Is it?

Chloë I'm using Kanebo oils.

Don I'm not bothered.

Chloë The oil goes directly into the bloodstream. That's why you'll feel more of a glow.

Chloë digs in to Don's back

Don That's a bit tender.

Chloë You've got a knotty back.

Don A nutty back?

Chloë Knotty.

Don That's about right.

Chloë I'm going to work the bottom of your back now.

Chloë walks to the head of the table. She smothers Don with her breasts, and begins to draw her hands up from the base of his spine

Chloë There we go.

Don Ohhhh.

Chloë Nice and firm.

Don (*loudly*) Ooohhhh.

Chloë Good?

Don (*loudly*) Orhhghhhh.

Chloë Could you just keep your voice down? We prefer discretion.

Don It is unbelievable.

Chloë Nice and slow.

Don This is legal, isn't it?

Chloë I think so. Nice?

Don Oh, yes, that is it, that's the spot. Oh yes. This is … Oh, dear …

Chloë Now I'm going to work up to your head.

Chloë massages Don's neck and pulls her hands into his hair. She pushes his face into the table. He can hardly breathe. He turns his face DS

Don I think that's a bit too firm.
Chloë Nice and firm.
Don You're breaking my nose.
Chloë Just relax.
Don I can't breathe.
Chloë Just let it all go ...
Don If only ...
Chloë Just relax — just relax ...
Don Arghhhhhhhh.
Chloë Relax.
Don Arghhhhhhhh.
Chloë Relaxxxxx ...
Chloë How's that feel?
Don Arghhhhh.
Chloë Better.
Don Ohhhhhh.
Chloë You remember this feeling?
Don Ohhhhh.
Chloë There we are.
Don You couldn't do it again for me, could you?
Chloë Not today.
Don (*almost speechless*) I'm in heaven.

Don climbs off the table. The towel is stuck down the back of his briefs

Chloë wheels the table off

Don turns; he is stranded on stage. He hobbles off

Music plays and the Lights fade

SCENE 3

The Relaxation Conservatory

A Bellboy enters and sets a number of chairs around a table — including the wicker chair. A number of large hanging baskets is flown in

The music fades

Ken enters, with a cup of tea

Bellboy Can I get you a coffee or anything, sir?
Ken Got one, thanks. You can book me another sunbed though, and tell them
I want the fast tan — I haven't got time for the other one. I was on it for that
long I felt like a kebab.
Bellboy I'll mention it at the treatment centre, sir.

The Bellboy exits

*Gertrude Tate enters. She is elderly, with a refined voice. She walks with
a stick*

Gertrude Someone's taken *The Times*; have you seen *The Times*?
Ken It's in the lounge.
Gertrude Oh, I'm not going back, darling. It's down there; I just can't be
bothered.
Ken Shall I?
Gertrude Oh, no, darling, I couldn't possibly ask you.
Ken It's no problem.
Gertrude No honestly ... erm ...?
Ken Ken.
Gertrude Ben?
Ken Ken.
Gertrude Ben who, darling?
Ken Ken Blake.
Gertrude Ken Blake. Hallo. Gertrude Tate.
Ken Hallo.
Gertrude Have I met you before?
Ken Yesterday.
Gertrude Ah good. I thought I had.
Ken Yes, we had a little chat about the vegan menu.
Gertrude Good, very good. I thought I had. Ben Blake. I remember you now.
Are you the one with the wife from Hong Kong?
Ken Not me, sadly.
Gertrude You're not the judge are you?
Ken 'Fraid not.
Gertrude Have you been here before?
Ken Once or twice.
Gertrude Oh good, very good. You're not the man with the jewels are you?
I spoke to him at the weekend. Fascinating. Did you go to his talk?
Ken No, I ...
Gertrude No, neither did I! Couldn't bear to listen to his voice — he had
quite a high voice, didn't he?
Ken I didn't meet him.
Gertrude You're not a first-timer, then?
Ken Oh, no.

Gertrude Can't stand these first-timers, love. Don't know why they bother coming to be honest. They only get under one's feet.

Ken You've been coming a lot then?

Gertrude Ben, I can remember Scardale when old Tony Mansfield had it. And that's going back a bit. So what treatments have you had?

Ken Just a massage so far. I tend to use the gym a lot.

Gertrude Have you had the Multi Method?

Ken No.

Gertrude Two girls pull you this way and that for an hour, Ben. It's quite wonderful.

Ken Sounds like a wrestling match.

Gertrude One feels quite stuffed at the end of it.

Ken Really.

Gertrude I felt like a blessed chicken, love.

Ken Oh no, I'd not fancy that.

Gertrude One of them nearly had my leg out of the socket.

Ken Really?

Gertrude I don't mind it a little firm, but one of them was so awkward, I said to her: "I'm not paying all this money to have my hip put out by a floosie from Loughborough".

Ken Could have been painful.

Gertrude It was. These new girls aren't what they were.

Ken Why, what were they?

Gertrude How much are they charging you?

Ken I'm on a package.

Gertrude We're all on packages, love ... How much, go on?

Ken One hundred and eighty a night.

Gertrude Very good, love.

Ken It's a ten-day package.

Gertrude Ben, I went on the Orient Express two years ago. Venice and back, love. Stayed at the *Cipriani*. Joan Collins was there. Did you read her book? I had one of those tapes ... Damn machine broke, Ben, and I never finished it. Six thousand pounds there and back. Never finished the tape, Ben, but let's be honest ...

Ken No, I don't really fancy rail travel.

Gertrude You been to Venice?

Ken No, I haven't actually.

Gertrude Six thousand pounds there and back.

Ken Not cheap.

Gertrude You get what you pay for.

Ken I tend to fly.

Gertrude Wonderful, wonderful place, but the water is quite filthy. The whole place is shrouded in a veil of death love. Wonderful for the elderly. I don't think I shall ever go back, really. You must go to the Guggenheim, if you're there ... My cousin met her, you know?

Shirley enters. She too wears a robe and looks fresher after her seaweed bath. She carries a bag and a mug of coffee. She sits down next to Gertrude

Shirley Hallo again. I think the aerobics are just about getting to me.
Ken You'll get used to it.
Shirley Isn't it fantastic?
Gertrude You know Ben, do you?
Shirley We met in the studio.
Ken Actually …
Gertrude And you are?
Shirley Shirley.
Gertrude From?
Shirley Buxton.
Gertrude Have we met before?
Shirley No, I don't think so.
Gertrude You're not the lesbian girl are you?
Shirley Oh no, not me.
Gertrude Born in Buxton?
Shirley No, born in Tring.
Gertrude It all goes in here, love. (*She indicates her head*)
Shirley I have two children.
Gertrude And?
Shirley That's it, really.
Gertrude Never had any time for children, love. Never had much time for sex, to be honest. It isn't all it's cracked up to be is it, Ben?
Ken Well … ?
Gertrude Too old now, love.
Ken I think it depends how you do it.
Gertrude Very good, Ben.
Shirley That's true.
Gertrude There are a lot more important things. More boring, but a lot more important.
Shirley Yes that's true as well.
Gertrude You here on your own are you?
Shirley No, with my husband.
Gertrude I told my husband I was going to Norway one year, and he said, "Who with?" and I said "The man at the end of the street." And he said, "You hardly know him." I said, "It's the travel agent, you great berk." Very funny, my marriage, I can tell you. Then he just said "Bloody well go then."
Shirley Oh, great.
Gertrude Wonderful man. Don't make 'em like that any more.
Shirley Broke the mould, did they?
Gertrude Are you going away? I was just saying Venice is so wonderful.
Shirley Yes, we're having a couple of days.

Gertrude At the Gritti Palace?
Shirley It's hardly a palace.
Gertrude At the *Cipriani*, love?
Shirley No, in a chalet.
Gertrude In Venice?
Shirley No, Bournemouth. Just for a week. The four of us.
Gertrude I wouldn't touch it with a bargepole love.
Shirley Oh, it's nice.
Gertrude Couldn't possibly face it, love.
Shirley Well, sometimes it gets a little bit cold at night.
Gertrude Awful, quite ghastly.
Shirley It's not too bad, there's a storage heater.
Gertrude Sounds horrendous.
Shirley Well, I don't really like it, but Don says it's all we can afford this year.
Gertrude I don't go on holiday in this country any more, it is just so vulgar.
Shirley We don't play the bingo.
Ken I would.
Shirley Well, the kids like it. They can fool about, can't they?
Gertrude And the English abroad? If we're not bad enough in this country we are even worse abroad. "Here they go, here they go." Slobs most of them. Football and beefburgers. The whole things seems to be a mess. What do you think, Ben?
Ken Well, I think the football's a mess.
Gertrude Sorry, Ben love, I know I go on; please stop me if I'm boring you, darling. I know you like to listen, love. He told me.
Ken Don't have much choice, do I?

Don enters. He is now dressed in a dressing-gown. His face is bright red, with marks all over it, and his hair is a real mess. He has just returned from his massage

Don Oh, dear ...
Shirley This is Don, my husband.
Don Ohh.
Ken What have you just had?
Don Back and neck.
Ken Good?
Don Ohhhh.
Gertrude Did you have the fat one?
Don Sorry?
Gertrude The fat one — did you have the fat girl?
Don No, she wasn't fat.
Gertrude She really gets into you, that one. You can feel her thighs pushing against the table, but she really makes it work.

Don I had Chloë. She's going on a cruise. I'm going with her.
Gertrude You're going on a cruise, are you?
Don No. We're going to Bournemouth.
Gertrude On a cruise?
Don No, in a chalet.
Shirley Feel good, then?
Don Better.
Gertrude How much is it?
Don Thirty-five quid, I think.
Gertrude A night?
Don The massage!
Gertrude How much is it a night?
Don The chalet in Bournemouth is three hundred for the fortnight!
Gertrude It sounds like a nightmare.
Don Yes, it is usually. Bloody kids all over the shop!
Gertrude How can you possibly stand it?
Don We were to the chalet born.
Gertrude What's the time, anyone? I've got aromatherapy at six.
Shirley Nearly a quarter to.
Gertrude Well, I'll leave you; probably bored you silly anyway.
Ken No, not at all.
Gertrude You're a nice man, Ben, even though I expected you to get me the paper.
Ken Catch you later.
Gertrude You know I should be careful about Bournemouth. A sister of mine went there years ago. Took ill.
Shirley Oh dear.
Gertrude She went into hospital and they took her kidney out.
Shirley Oh well.
Gertrude She never got better. Bye bye.

And in a moment Gertrude has gone

Don You get 'em all in here.
Shirley I feel sorry for her. I mean she's obviously lonely.
Don There's no wonder if she keeps coming out with such bollocks.
Shirley Honestly just ignore him, Ben — I'm sorry, I thought it was Ken.
Ken It is Ken.
Shirley Oh sorry, I thought she said Ben ...
Ken She did, but ——
Don (*reclining in a chair*) I am completely done for.
Ken You'll not fancy a game of squash then?
Don Not at the moment.
Ken Pity, I'm looking for a partner.

Don I couldn't pick the racquet up.
Ken I'll give you a game if you fancy one.
Shirley Don's not much of a sporty type any more.
Ken Well, he's in the wrong place.
Don I feel like I'm in the right place.
Ken Have you ever played?
Don I've played table tennis.
Shirley Well, that's nearly the same isn't it?
Don Yeah, it's nearly the same, except for the fact that it's completely different.
Ken This your first time?
Shirley Yeah. You come a lot, do you?
Ken When I can.
Shirley It's a bit pricey though.
Don What line of work are you in?
Ken Building. You?
Don I design kitchens.
Ken Pity, I've just had mine done. Business booming?
Don Well. You?
Ken Very nice at the moment. Right, if you'll excuse me I'll go and have a session with Zoë in the gym. Don't fancy that, do you?
Don Not at the moment; I'm going to have my cup of camomile tea and then have a lie down.
Ken See you about.

Ken departs

Silence

Shirley Nice bloke.
Don If you like testosterone.
Shirley You should play him at squash. You used to play, didn't you?
Don I'll just read or something.
Shirley Are you OK?
Don I just feel a bit light-headed to be honest.
Shirley It's because you're thinking about it.
Don I am not thinking about it; I am just sat here, relaxing. In fact I'm not thinking about anything.
Shirley I bet you didn't feel light-headed in the massage.
Don Have you got a paracetamol or something? I've got a splitting head.
Shirley In my bag.

Don grabs the bag that Shirley has brought in with her and has a rummage around. He finds a small booklet

Don What's this?
Shirley Oh it's a free book I got with *New Women*.
Don "Close Up. Erotic Literature for Women"?
Shirley It came with the magazine.
Don Oh, right.
Shirley Oh, honestly?
Don You're not reading it, are you?
Shirley No, I'm eating it.
Don So they're pumping all this stuff at women now are they?
Shirley I'm only reading it for something to do, so don't hold that against me.
Don (*opening the book and reading*) "She cast aside conventional love-making and was overtaken by wanton desire."
Shirley You've never read anything like it, have you?
Don Well, it didn't come free. What are you reading this stuff for?
Shirley I'm just reading it.

A beat

So you feel better for the massage?
Don One massage isn't going to make a difference, love.
Shirley Don't call me love.
Don Sorry.
Shirley Don't call me love.
Don I said I was sorry.
Shirley So at the end of the week you've decided that you're not going to feel any less stressed?
Don Please!
Shirley Oh, stop it.
Don You want to know how I feel?
Shirley I know how you feel ——

Chloë enters US, and crosses the stage

Chloë (*to Shirley, whispering*) Hallo.
Shirley (*disturbed in full flow; whispering*) Hallo.

Chloë exits

(*To Don*) You tell me about the pains in your arms or the twitches in your head. You tell me your every bodily function.
Don A month ago, right, at my mother's, I looked at my hands and I couldn't recognize my hands. I looked and I thought "Shit, these aren't my hands!"
Shirley So we're here and we're doing something about it.

Don Have you any idea how much we're owed?
Shirley Oh, don't start going on about money — I can't bear it!
Don You never want to hear about it.
Shirley And you never do anything to help yourself. You never relax.
Don No, because I've got the time, haven't I?
Shirley I mean you never take breaks. We haven't been away together for
  months, a year nearly. If you ask me you're in the wrong job.
Don Oh, helpful.
Shirley Well you are!
Don Very helpful.
Shirley You just won't admit it.
Don I'll pack it in then. In fact, I've packed it in. I am no longer involved with
  a kitchen firm. I am now a round the world yachtswoman. Wow, feels a lot
  better already.
Shirley It's non-creative, that's the trouble.
Don "Yes, we had a lovely day at sea today. Lost three crew but by God it's
  so bracing!"
Shirley See what I mean?
Don Fancy saying I'm in the wrong job.

Shaun drifts on US

Shaun Do you know what film is on tonight?
Shirley No sorry.
Shaun It's that Jack Nicholson thing. Why don't they show something that
  young people might enjoy?
Don Hey, don't worry about it.
Shaun I'm not.
Don Well, don't look back in anger.
Shaun Is that supposed to be a joke?
Don My son loves that stuff: Oasis!
Shaun Oh, wow, a funny man.
Don I'm sorry, I didn't mean to be ——
Shaun I've been trying to get on a squash court for three hours, I'm not in
  the mood, all right?

Shaun exits

Don Salt of the earth.
Shirley Angry young man.
Shirley You were once.
Don I'm not angry any more. I haven't got the energy.
Shirley You will be in a minute.
Don Why?

Shirley There's no wine on the menu. Apparently, they have one day on alcohol, and two days off.

Don So I can't have a drink?

Shirley Tonight's an off night.

Don You're joking?

Shirley And on the nights on, you're only allowed two units.

Don (*shocked*) That is insane, and all the money we're paying? I bet they had a drink in bloody Colditz!

Shirley You've got a drink problem.

Don I will have tonight!

Shirley You haven't had a night without booze for ten years! Probably longer!

Don Three units a day we're supposed to have, everybody knows that. It's good for your heart.

Shirley But you have nine.

Don I'm taking extra precautions.

Shirley That's why you're stressed, you drink too much.

Don I can't face reality without a drink.

Shirley You won't admit it.

Don Why are you stressed, then? You don't drink at all?

Shirley I don't drink as much as you.

A beat. Silence

Don Anyway, there's no problem, I'll nip down to that offie I saw in the village.

Shirley You won't.

Don I will.

Shirley They don't allow you off the campus after six!

Don Eh?

Shirley And they compound all the cars.

Don Wonderful.

Shirley That's what they told me at the seaweed bath.

Don Great.

Shirley It'll be nice to just be together and relax; you never know what might happen.

Don Can't have a drink, you can't go out, there's nothing to eat and they lock you in your bedrooms. I wondered what the bars were doing on the walls. I thought at first it was a design feature.

A beat

Shirley Why do you always need a drink before you make love to me, anyway?

Don I don't.
Shirley Even at college you did.
Don Everybody does.
Shirley Everybody did at college.
Don They still do.
Shirley I don't. Maxine's Thomas doesn't.
Don So that's what you talk about when she comes round, is it?
Shirley I've got to talk to somebody.
Don Well, he's lucky then. I just do, it gets me more in the mood.
Shirley Oh, come on.
Don It does.
Shirley You can't say that, we haven't done anything for two years.
Don We have.
Shirley You haven't made love to me for two years.
Don I hope you didn't tell Maxine that.
Shirley Why, would you like to make love to her?
Don Not particularly.
Shirley You fancy all my friends.
Don I don't.
Shirley You fancy Maxine.
Don I don't fancy Annette and June.
Shirley June's sixty-eight.
Don Is she?
Shirley So would you like to sleep with Maxine?
Don You ought to stop reading that erotic literature; it's making you sex mad.
Shirley So why don't you want to make love to me then?
Don I don't feel confident about myself.
Shirley But you'd feel confident with Maxine?
Don I don't know where this has come from.
Shirley Is it me? I mean I've been on a diet for two years.
Don I know that, but you've only lost four pounds, that's not a diet, Shirl.
    If we're being honest, be honest with yourself.
Shirley I happen to be taking it steady.
Don I drink, you eat; that's quite a balanced thing.
Shirley So you don't like me this shape.
Don Forget it.
Shirley No, I want to know.
Don What do you want me to say? No, love, you're not Christie Brinkley.
Shirley Don't call me love.
Don What do you want me to say?
Shirley Don, I'm thirty-seven, I'm not a little girl. I know I've got fat legs,
    my mother has. I wish I could cut the sodding things off.
Don You haven't got fat legs. How many times do I have to tell you?
Shirley You never tell the truth.

Ken enters; he has come from the gym

Ken I was going to have a decent workout, but I've broken the rower.
Don That's another thousand quid on your bill then.
Ken You should've seen me. Took my heart rate up to two hundred and four.
Don You want to be careful you don't explode.
Ken Anybody fancy a race in the pool?
Don Not for me.
Ken What about my aerobics partner?
Shirley (*definitely*) No! (*Softer*) Sorry, I'm not really into swimming.
Ken Why not?
Shirley I just don't feel ——
Don You go if you want.
Ken Come on, we can do a few lengths. I promise not to drown you.
Shirley No, I don't want to.
Ken Not shy, are you?
Shirley I don't feel ——
Ken We can just swim up and down, have a natter? Come on, get your kit
  on; leave him, let him drift away with the fairies.
Don Go and have a swim if you want one.
Ken I think there's an Aqua Tone class on in the big pool — we could do that.
Shirley I'll have to go and get my costume.
Ken Well, go on then. You don't mind, do you?
Don No, not at all.
Shirley I'll go and get my stuff then, shall I?

Shirley departs, taking her bag with her

The two men are left alone for a moment

Ken Enjoying it, are you?
Don I would be if I could have a drink.
Ken I'm teetotal. I don't touch the stuff. It rots your body. What is it then,
  a sort of second honeymoon? Quite a few people do it these days. What
  room are you in?
Don Twenty-seven.
Ken I'm in twenty-eight.
Don Next door then.
Ken I promise not to listen.
Don Yeah, you never know what you might hear.
Ken What have you got lined up tomorrow, then?
Don I was just looking at this. I might have my colours done.
Ken Get on the squash court; there's nothing like it.

Don You're a fit bloke; look at me, I'm on my last legs.

Ken How old are you?

Don Forty on Thursday.

Ken I was forty-two in January.

Don You. Never.

Ken Good living, mate.

Don Good something.

Ken So what do you reckon to the massages, then? A bit of all right, isn't it?
Did you strip right down?

Don To my underwear.

Ken Yesterday, I took it all off. Just to see what they'd do. Didn't get
anything, but you should've seen the look on her face.

Don I bet.

Ken Mind you, I could do something for that Zoë eh?

Don Well, I …

Ken Fit?

Don I wouldn't know where to start. Not in that league I'm afraid.

Ken You ever been to Thailand?

Don No, we go to Flamingo Land though.

Ken Couple of quid and you're laughing there, mate. Mind you the food's
absolute rubbish.

Don Yeah. It is at Flamingo Land.

Ken The food here is exquisite, none of your Paki stuff or pizzas here, mate.

Don Oh, I don't mind it.

Ken Get off, it's absolute garbage. I don't touch any of that stuff. I don't eat
any foreign muck. Garbage.

Don So is a full English breakfast.

Ken Anyway, I'll see you later.

Don Hey, don't let her get drowned, will you? She's not the best swimmer
in the world.

Ken She's safe in my hands.

Don Yeah, that's what they said about the National Health Service.

Ken exits

Don stretches and walks around the room for a while

Gertrude enters with a newspaper

Gertrude Found the blessed paper love, and then somebody had already
done the crossword. Most of it wrong, I have to say. First-timers, I bet you.
And if that's not bad enough the silly girl had got me in for the wrong
treatment. Oh, sorry, I thought you were Ben.

Don Ben?

Gertrude The one with the aftershave.

Don Ken?

Gertrude Not Ken, Ben, love — Ben.

Don Not seen a Ben. Ken's taking my wife for a swim.

Gertrude I used to take the dog for a walk — damn thing it was, bit me twice. Had to put it down at the end of the day. Sad really. Do you like setters?

Don No, I'm not much of an animal lover.

Gertrude Always loved animals, love, any shape or size. My father kept a llama. Never really knew why.

Don I had a goldfish when I was five, but that was it for me. And that died on me.

Gertrude That's the drawback, darling, they do. They die before you do. Sad really.

Don It is.

Gertrude And you are?

Don Me?

Gertrude Hallo Me; have we met?

Don Not officially.

Gertrude You're not the man with the wife from Hong Kong, are you?

Don No she's originally from Tring!

Gertrude Tring?

Don Hallo.

Gertrude Sorry.

Don Wrong number.

Gertrude Sorry?

Don I was being facetious.

Gertrude (*referring to her paper*) The country's going to the dogs, love. but there you go. What can we do?

Don Well, I don't know if that's true.

Gertrude Nothing! Absolutely nothing!

Don No, right.

Gertrude We all thought very different once, love, but it's gone too far. No-one has any respect for those sad little politicians' lies any more. So we hide away in here for weeks on end, keep our heads down. You're not the MP by the way, are you?

Don Not me!

Gertrude Oh good, love, well you're not the judge are you?

Don No, I'm into kitchens.

Gertrude Oh, a plumber?

Don That's right.

Gertrude Well, the tap in my bedroom's leaking a little.

Don I came here to relax.

Gertrude We all have. We're all here to find ourselves.
Don I can't switch off.
Gertrude Just like my tap, love.
Don I haven't done for ten years.
Gertrude I have the opposite trouble, love, I can't switch on . But I do try everything, love, to keep the old ticker ——
Don I don't want to overdo it.
Gertrude Give yourself up to it, love; it's the only way to let go of stress.
Don I do let go, but then another stress jumps on me!
Gertrude Vicious circle, love.
Don My wife says I'm too negative.
Gertrude Lugubrious, love. I can sense it from you. Well, I suppose I'd better go for my manicure before they send out another search party.
Don Life's full of little troubles, isn't it?
Gertrude Darling, I'm seventy-one and everything's a battle for me. But I'm not giving in. (*She struggles to her feet and moves behind Don*)
Don Good for you!
Gertrude "Like as the waves make towards the pebbled shore, So do our minutes hasten to their end." Well, I've enjoyed our little chat. I haven't talked to a plumber for years. Not bad at all really. Bye bye.
Don Life doesn't get any simpler as you get older then?
Gertrude Darling, life is a turd sandwich and then you die — didn't you know?

Music plays. The Lights fade

Don stands and hobbles off

The Bellboy enters and strikes the seating, except the wicker chair

SCENE 4

Aerobics Studio

Zoë is sorting out some Reebok slide equipment — slide mats and special slippery covers for trainers —from the cupboard. She has her cassette player with her

The music fades

Ken enters

Zoë Hiya.

Ken How you doing?
Zoë Great. How are you?
Ken Feeling brilliant at the moment.
Zoë Really?
Ken So this is hard, is it?
Zoë It's a killer. Good for the inner thigh, though.
Ken I bet it is.
Zoë How did you get on with the stepper?
Ken Took my heart up to two hundred and ten.
Zoë What are you training for?
Ken Life.
Zoë Sounds ominous.
Ken Yes, my knees were bleeding but I reached level twelve. Tomorrow, level thirteen, the ultimate test. I like to see that little man jump up and down on the computer thing. It's the only thing that keeps me going. (*He looks off*) Here she is!

Shirley enters

Shirley Hiya.
Ken How you doing?
Shirley I'm a bit stiff today.
Zoë This'll sort you out.
Shirley I did the morning walk. Isn't it wonderful countryside? And the fresh air ... I mean, I thought we had fresh air but ...
Ken So you'll be coming again then?
Shirley I've got to change my lifestyle; that's what they said at the talk on stress. We've all got palæolithic bodies apparently. I think I know how that feels.
Zoë How's the weight going?
Shirley Half a pound overnight. I can't believe it. I got on the scales this morning and I thought they were out, but no, there it was in black and white. Mind you, I only had a nibble last night. I am starving.
Ken Can we talk about something else?
Shirley I could eat a horse, to be honest.
Zoë You got a nice room?
Shirley It's lovely, but Don couldn't sleep.
Ken I thought I heard some moaning.
Shirley Did you hear him shouting?
Zoë Those rooms are too warm.
Shirley That didn't help. He was going up the walls. First night without a drop of alcohol in ten years. I thought he was going to blow up. He was up until five reading, so now he says he's more stressed out than when we arrived.

Ken He's probably right.
Shirley Mind you he was up at seven; said he was going to the gym.
Ken Getting into it then!
Shirley Well, we'll see. Then he booked to have his colours done.
Ken He'll be fit if he keeps that up.
Shirley He'll not keep it up. He bought one of them rower things once. He never goes on it. He says it makes him seasick.

Don enters. He is wearing a bright lime top, and has a heart rate monitor on his wrist

Zoë I thought you might be avoiding us.
Don Why, it's not too hard, is it?
Shirley What are you wearing?
Don I've just bought it. Monique said lime was one of my colours.
Ken Are you sure?
Don I'm sure she said lime. Treated myself to one from the boutique. And I've got myself this. (*He checks his new toy, the heart monitor*) Heart monitor. So you can judge your optimum heart work rate. Apparently I should get my heart to do one hundred and forty beats per minute for twenty minutes three times a week.
Zoë That's very good.
Shirley What's it doing now?
Don (*looking at his wrist*) Nothing.
Ken You're dead then.
Don I must be. Shit. Oh, hang on, I've not turned it on yet.
Ken Lucky let-off.
Don These are the latest thing. I'm surprised you've not got one, Ken?
Zoë OK, slide is the latest aerobic exercise which gives you fantastic burn; it's a low-impact high-cardio workout. The idea is, that you push with your legs and slide from one side of the pad to the other. So, if you'd like to put the shoes on ...

Shirley, Ken and Don fix the special shoe covers to the bottoms of their trainers; they are very slippery. They walk to their slide mats. Ken and Shirley do quite well but Don cannot keep his feet; the image is funny and pathetic. With some difficulty, he eventually gets to his slide mat

Don Who's thought this bloody thing up?
Zoë It's the latest thing.

Don finally gets on to his slide mat

OK we're going to slide one way then another way. Very simple. Let's go with the music.

Zoë switches on her cassette player; music plays. The others follow her instructions

OK, with the music. Step, and slide over, then push and slide over, and step — that's good — and slide over. That's real nice. Let's get a rhythm. Well done, Ken; nice one, Shirley — and step and slide over. Keep at it, Don.

Don I can't get the step.

Ken Just relax, you're too tense.

Don I can't stand up.

Ken It's easy, watch.

Don This is insane.

Zoë Keep stepping and slide, Don. Just push away.

Ken What's your heart doing?

Don (*looking at his heart monitor*) One hundred and twenty.

Ken You're unfit, mate.

Don It's not the exercise, it's the concentration.

Zoë That's good, Shirley; think about that inner thigh.

Shirley I'm thinking about my inner thigh, my rear end — everything.

Don One hundred and forty now!

Ken Yeah, you've just got to keep that up for twenty minutes.

Don What, like this?

Zoë Keep sliding, Don.

Don Can't do much else with these on your feet can you?

Zoë Concentrate on the glide.

Don Why am I here?

Ken Only another nineteen minutes and thirty seconds.

Don I feel like I'm doing the bloody Riverdance.

Zoë Concentrate, Don.

Don One hundred and seventy. One hundred and seventy.

Shirley Are you sure?

Zoë Wow, OK, hold it.

Don Stop! Wow stop. Shit, I can't get my breath. (*He steps off the mat. He is all over the place, breathing heavily, unable to get his breath*)

Zoë makes for the cassette and switches off the music

Zoë Sit, just sit.

Don Oh, my chest. Jesus, my chest's tight.

Zoë Just relax.

Don One hundred and ninety-two?

Shirley Just breathe, relax.

Don Oh, God, Shirley.

Ken Just take it easy; just relax, mate.

Don Oh, Shirl. Pains in my chest. Honestly — tightness all across my chest and down my arms. This is it, Shirl. I'm bloody going.
Shirley Hang on, hang on, relax … He's having a panic attack.
Zoë I'll get you a cup of water.

Zoë exits

Shirley and Ken comfort Don

Don Will I be all right, Shirl?
Ken He doesn't want mouth to mouth, does he?
Don Not with you.
Shirley OK, it's OK.
Don I've got myself all wound up.
Shirley Just relax.
Don Is it going down?
Ken (*looking at the monitor*) A hundred and seventy still.
Shirley He gets himself into a state, can't let go, and suddenly he's thrown into a panic do.
Ken Just breathe nice and deep.
Don I'm sorry.
Shirley It's OK.
Don Sorry.

Gertrude enters US. *She is lost once more*

Gertrude I'm looking for the Indian head massage? Is it in here? Down beyond the treatment rooms they said. Well, I went and I couldn't see anybody vaguely Eastern in there. Is it that little man who's doing it? I can hardly make out anything he says most of the time. I went to hear his talk about T'ai Ch'i and I thought he was talking about a blessed panda for twenty minutes, love. What's going on in here, then, first aid?
Shirley That's right.
Gertrude Very good, love. You never know when you might need it. I'll try the art room, you never know your luck!

Gertrude exits

Zoë returns with a glass of water

Zoë Feeling any better?
Don Thanks, sorry.
Zoë No problem.

Ken It seems to be settling down. A hundred and fifteen now. Have you seen a doctor?

Shirley He's seen everybody there is to see. It's all upstairs, they said, in his head.

Don My heart's not in my head, is it? It's in my chest. Mind you, I thought it was coming out of the top of my bloody skull, then.

Ken We'd hardly got going.

Don I was determined to get into it and all.

Ken Pity, I just fancied a real good sweat.

Don I really am terribly embarrassed.

Zoë You don't need the nurse, do you?

Don No, I think I've got it under control.

Zoë Do you want any more water?

Don No, I'm fine, thanks.

Zoë Are you sure?

Don Yes, I'm fine, thanks. Shit. Sorry.

Zoë What have you got next?

Don I've got something in an hour — massage I think.

Shirley Why don't you go and lay down, and then go for a massage?

Zoë Shall we go and have some fresh air?

Shirley So you want me to ——

Don No, you stay here, no good you getting all changed.

Zoë We'll just get a bit of fresh air and then he should be fine. We'll have to call that it. Do it tomorrow.

Ken No problem.

Don Sorry, sorry; I feel bloody pathetic.

Ken Don't worry about it. It must be your age.

Don Thanks.

Ken It was a joke, mate.

Shirley Do you remember jokes, Don?

Don Just about.

Zoë I said it was a killer.

Don gets to his feet

Shirley Do you want us to do anything with all this stuff?

Zoë Just put it to one side, if you don't mind.

Shirley You OK, Don?

Don Fine, now. (*He takes a reading*) It's back to ninety-four.

Ken I don't think the lime T-shirt helped.

Shirley No, don't go out in that for God's sake!

Zoë and Don exit

Shirley and Ken tidy up the slide equipment during the following

Ken Does it happen a lot?
Shirley He's too highly strung.
Ken He seems OK now.
Shirley One minute he's OK, then he's having a panic.
Ken Why does he get wound up?
Shirley That's the sixty-four thousand dollar question. He lost his dad last
   year and they were very close, then his mum had a funny do. They thought
   she'd got angina, so they put her on these tablets which expand your
   arteries. They were making her go blind.
Ken Oh, lovely.
Shirley Finally Don paid for her to go private.
Ken Angiogram — my dad's had one.
Shirley There's nothing wrong with her heart apparently. It was all
   psychosomatic. And he's got this thing about being forty. And then there's
   work. I mean, we're not poor, but this is a special treat really.
Ken Hence the chalet in Bournemouth?
Shirley I don't know why he ever went into business, he hasn't got the right
   sort of mentality. He did English at university and he's ended up running
   a kitchen firm.
Ken From the sublime to the ridiculous.
Shirley Oh, I know, doesn't it sound crazy? His uncle left this little firm to
   him and his dad. So Don stopped his MA course and went into selling fitted
   kitchens. We used to laugh about it. He said one day he would write a book
   about it. His dad was an electrician on the assembly line at Rover. Neither
   of them knew the first thing about business. His mother talked him into
   doing it; she thought it would offer job security. I think he regrets it, really,
   but we're mortgaged to death, so ... You can't turn the clock back, though,
   can you?
Ken That sounds a bit grim.
Shirley We were going to do all sorts but I fell pregnant.
Ken That's a weird phrase, isn't it?
Shirley Yeah, I suppose it is.
Ken It sounds like some sort of accident in the garden.
Shirley It was.
Ken What?
Shirley An accident in the garden. It was at my mother's; we didn't plan for
   it. We didn't plan for anything then.
Ken The good old days?
Shirley Things were a lot simpler.
Ken And boring probably?
Shirley No, not boring then. Boring now. Now we don't go to the shops
   unless we've got a plan. He has to write everything down or he forgets.

Ken Come on, I'll buy you a peppermint tea.
Shirley No, I'm fine, really.
Ken Come on, it sounds like you need something.
Shirley I need a lot of things.
Ken Make a wish.
Shirley What I really need is a big piece of chocolate cake.
Ken Well, that's easily arranged.
Shirley And two weeks of mindless sex.
Ken Excuse me?
Shirley Sorry.
Ken I think that's what everyone needs, don't you?
Shirley I shouldn't've said that, should I?
Ken Well, it's not the usual conversation here.
Shirley Just thinking aloud.
Ken You've got Don, haven't you?
Shirley That's right.
Ken Well, erm …
Shirley Look, I, erm — just say the first thing that comes into my head
sometimes.
Ken Tell you what, if you're good I'll treat you to the next best thing.
Shirley Oh yeah, and what's that?
Ken A flapjack!
Shirley Yeah, go on then, I'll settle for a flapjack today.

Music plays. The Lights fade

Ken and Shirley exit together chatting easily

SCENE 5

Treatment Room

Don enters US. *He sits in the wicker chair and awaits his next treatment*

*Chloë wheels on the massage table. She is dressed in her white smock as
before*

The music fades

Don moves to Chloë. He is still a little bit shaken

Chloë How are we today?
Don Not too bad, I nearly had a stroke in the aerobic session, but apart from
that I'm fine, and my heart's doing a steady eighty-two at the moment.

Chloë Well, this should be just what you're looking for.
Don Shall I get ready?
Chloë Please.

Don gets undressed during the following

Don I went to the slide class.
Chloë Hard work?
Don Have you ever done it?
Chloë No, I'm a bit of a couch potato when it comes to exercise.
Don Don't mention food, Chloë, if you don't mind; I could eat one of the squirrels in the park.
Chloë Hungry.
Don I think I've gone beyond hunger. I'm actually hallucinating now. If I froth at the mouth give me another stick of celery. *(By now he is down to his underpants)* Right then. All ready.
Chloë It's just a facial, isn't it?
Don Is it?
Chloë You needn't have stripped down.
Don Oh.
Chloë Would you like to put your clothes back on?
Don Well, actually, I'd prefer to have it like this if it's all right with you?
Chloë Fine. Would you like to get on the couch? Face up.
Don Yeah, I think I've got that. *(He gets on the table)*

Chloë covers Don's underpants with a white towel

Chloë Would prefer me to use Decleor or Clarins?
Don I haven't got a clue. Use mud if you want.
Chloë Do you put much on your face?
Don Only egg.
Chloë Oh, good, like an egg wash?
Don That's right.
Chloë I'm going to cleanse and soothe first of all, then I'll massage it with a revitalizing oil.
Don Yeah, then put a bag on my head, will you … ?
Chloë *(massaging Don's face)* How's that … ?
Don That's wonderful.
Chloë Hands not too cold?
Don No, fantastic.
Chloë This should soothe and cleanse.
Don I can feel it doing just that.
Chloë So just lay back and relax.

Don Try and stop me.
Chloë Just relax.
Don Ohhhhhh.
Chloë Reeeelaxxxx.
Don Ohhhh.
Chloë Relax ... .

Chloë massages Don's forehead and temples

The Lights fade and music plays — "O mio babbino cara" by Puccini

SCENE 6

Fantasy/Nightmare

The music continues under the following scene

The Lights give the effect of a nightmare

Don is still on the table

Sam, Don's son, enters, shouting wildly. Although played by a teenager he is dressed as a two-year-old

Sam Dad? Dad?
Don Not now, Sam, son.
Sam No way, no way, am I going to Bournemouth.

Shirley enters, from another direction. She is a nightmare vision of what we have previously seen

Shirley Can you have a word with her? She's wearing that skirt again, just look at what she looks like.
Don Don't let her wear it.
Sam In a chalet for a fortnight with him.
Shirley I don't know how we're supposed to live there's nothing coming in!
Don Don't shout, Shirley!

Maggie, Don's mother, enters. She is attached to a drip on wheels and looks like a ghost

Maggie I've made a cake, Don.
Don Mum, you shouldn't have!

Maggie I've made a cake for your party and we'll have jelly, and custard.
Sam Why can't I go to France with the others, Dad? Dad?
Maggie And we'll play musical chairs.
Sam Mum, why is he in the toilet all the time?
Maggie Such a lovely birthday. And I had pains in my chest all the time but I never told him.
Don Mum?

Maggie exits singing "Happy Birthday"

Mum?

During the following Chloë undresses herself and climbs on to the table with Don. The CURTAIN *very slowly falls as the scene progresses*

Chloë Is there anything else I can get you, Don?
Sam Dad, Holly's got a boyfriend.
Shirley Don, have you moved my pile cream?

Ken enters carrying a squash racquet

Ken Come on, Shirley, I've got a court booked.
Sam Dad, the goldfish is dead.
Ken It's all right isn't it, Don?
Shirley My mother's coming bank holiday. And you know she doesn't like lamb so we'll have to have pork.
Don I hate pork.
Sam What shall I do with it?
Shirley I know you hate pork but you'll just have to stomach it.
Don I can't stomach pork.
Ken What was she like at university, Don?
Don I'd rather have sausage.
Shirley It's pork sausage.
Sam Dad, there's cat shit on the car again!
Ken Don't overdo it, Don.
Sam Can I go to see Oasis?
Ken Don?
Sam Dad?

Maggie enters

Maggie I don't feel too well.
Chloë You must have had so many women.

Shirley Two years! It's not natural.
Ken Don!
Maggie Don!
Sam Dad?
Chloë What are you waiting for?
Shirley Don, the washer's broke and there's water all over the kitchen! Don, will you please come out of the toilet and sort this out ... DON! DON! DON!
Don Arghhhhhh!

The CURTAIN *falls, finally appearing to trap the action on stage*

ACT II
Scene 1

Squash Court

The Curtain *rises on darkness. In the darkness we can hear the violent grunts of two men, one more masculine. The noise is very loud and could be mistaken for a massage or sex*

The Lights quickly snap up to reveal Ken and Don, both in squash whites, sweating heavily, Don more than Ken. They are playing squash in the DS area against the imaginary fourth wall, and with an imaginary ball. Their bags and towels are nearby

We watch for a few moments as they make difficult and stress-making shots. Don is working very hard. Ken makes a point-winning shot. Suddenly the two men both stop, and all we can hear is them breathing heavily

Ken (*shouting at himself*) No, no, no! Hopeless, absolutely hopeless. Now come on. Fight, work for it. Let's go Ken, let's get straight back and eat him.
Don Steady on.
Ken Come on!

Don serves; Ken wins the point back

Don What's the score?
Ken Eh?
Don What score is it?
Ken It's match point. Two games to nil, twenty-nil, match point. Don, mate, you haven't scored a point.
Don I have, haven't I?
Ken No, this is what I'm saying. You have to score a point to win your serve. You can only score when you're serving.
Don Well, you haven't won yet, have you?
Ken So, what're you going to do — stage a comeback?
Don Come on!
Ken You're not going to have a panic, are you?
Don (*consulting his monitor*) A hundred and ten, and rising.
Ken It was a hundred when we started.
Don That must have been anticipation!

Ken I don't want to be responsible for you passing out.
Don Why, do I look flushed?
Ken Here we go, you ready?

Ken nonchalantly makes a shot. Don tries to dash for it but cannot prevent it being the winning point

Ken And the winner is ...
Don Bollocks, lucky ... That's it for me, I'm not playing any more, ever. My fingers are tingling.

Don and Ken shake hands. Don sits on the floor of the court

Ken Your ears are red as well. I should watch that, it might be something contagious.
Don Oh, what I wouldn't do for a nice glass of red.
Ken It's never interested me, that.
Don I used to drink boxes of the stuff. You know the boxes you can get?
Ken Think of your guts, mate.
Don I used to have a box a night. The next morning I'd get up and discover that I'd actually pulled the insides of the box out and wrung it dry. I was that desperate to get the last drop.
Ken I bet that went down well!

Don lays back and breaths deep and long

Shaun enters US. *He carries a squash racket*

Shaun How long are you going to be?
Ken Another hour.
Don I thought we'd finished?
Shaun All the other courts are booked.
Ken I'll give you a game after if you want?
Shaun No, thanks, I don't want annihilating. I only want to play because I'm bored. I'll go and have another steam bath. Hey, you look really red, mate.
Don Who me?
Shaun Don't overdo it, will you? The doctor's on holiday this week.
Don Is that supposed to be funny?
Shaun Yeah, why?
Don Well it's not, all right?
Shaun Careful, Grandad, don't have a stroke.
Don (*brandishing his racket*) I'll stroke you across the head with this in a minute.
Shaun Oh, will you?

Don Well, er …
Shaun I'd like to see you try.
Ken Hey, hey, gentlemen, gentlemen, please.
Don Sorry, sorry.

Shaun exits

Don Sorry, I, erm …
Ken Bloody hell, relax.

A beat. They towel down

Don So what's your story, Ken? You married then?
Ken Three times.
Don Woophh. Kids?
Ken No, sadly. You've got two haven't you?
Don Yes, Sam's a pain in the bum, but I can deal with him. But Holly, oh
  dear, fifteen and I haven't got a chance. The other week we'd gone to
  Sheffield, all four of us. I saw this young bloke looking at Holly. She's
  wearing an excuse for a skirt. I told Shirley not to let her put it on. But, no,
  she had to wear it. I could see what he was thinking.
Ken Achilles' heel, mate.
Don It was that look. It's the look he's got. (*He indicates Shaun*)
Ken It's human nature, isn't it?
Don Shirley didn't sense a thing. She's got no idea of danger. Bloody Holly
  thought it was great.
Ken Sounds like kids might be a no-no!
Don I'd got a kid in a Micra up my tail on Sunday.
Ken You're a victim, Don.
Don I'm beginning to wonder.
Ken They say it's how you wear yourself.
Don I was bringing my mother over to babysit.
Ken You're full of 'em, aren't you?
Don Flashing his lights — right up my backside, he was. So I pulled over to
  let him past, and he pulls behind me. So I pulls into the slow lane and there
  he is behind me, laughing like hell. I've got my mother in the back going
  on about her knicker elastic being too tight and the Knight Rider up my
  arse. So I pulled off the road near Birmingham, and the little sod pulled off
  as well. So I pulls into a lay-by and so does he. He gets out of the car and
  comes up to me. I mean, I am sweating, and by this time my mother's
  chosen topic has changed to bowel cancer. So I just sat in the car, he comes
  up to the window, spat on it, laughed at me and got back in his car and drove
  off giving me the finger. I mean, what was that all about?

Ken I told you, mate. It's a bloody jungle out there, you've got to be like Tarzan to survive.

Don Is that who you model yourself on?

Ken Yeah, my elephant is parked around the back.

Don And Shirley is just oblivious to it.

Ken She makes me smile, does your wife.

Don How do you mean?

Ken She comes out with some stuff.

Don What do you mean?

Ken Well, she comes out with some peculiar things.

Don Why, what's she been saying?

Ken I don't want to get her into any trouble. It was just a joke anyway.

Don What was it?

Ken The other day we'd got talking and she told me what she fancied most in the whole wide world. She's obviously not getting enough.

Don Enough of what?

Ken She told me she fancied two weeks of mindless sex.

Don Eh?

Ken That's what she said.

Don Who with?

Ken You, I suppose.

Don Oh, right.

Ken I asked her if she'd settle for a flapjack.

Don See what I mean Ken — men are evil!

Ken Anyway. Thanks for the game.

Don Thanks for the lesson in humiliation.

Ken No problem, anytime.

Don stands; he is quite stiff

Zoë enters; she is ready to play squash

Zoë So who won?

Don Guess.

Zoë You did?

Don Guess again.

Zoë A draw?

Ken Come on, then, let's see what you're made of.

Don You're not playing again, are you?

Zoë Course he is. I'm going to thrash him, and make him beg me to let him win.

Don Well, it's all in the wrist action apparently.

Zoë So they say.

Ken Competition, Don. It's what keeps you going. Success is a mind game.

Don collects his towel and bag and eases his way out of the court during the following

Don I've had my mind game for today. I'm going to have to get something to eat — I'm starving.
Zoë You were just the starter course, Don.
Ken That's right; you were just the warm-up man.
Don Funny that. I've been told that before.
Ken I would never have guessed.
Don In bed unfortunately.

Don exits

Ken and Zoë share a laugh at Don's expense. Ken has a slight pain in his chest. Zoë prepares to play

Ken and Zoë play. The Lights fade; we hear their grunting and the ball smashing against the wall

Music plays

Black-out

Ken and Zoë exit

Scene 2

Outside the Hall

It is a warm midsummer night

Small trees, a fountain, secluded seats and garden furniture adorn the stage. A swing is flown in

Shaun is hidden behind a small shrub, having a sly cigarette

The music fades

Shirley enters and breathes in the warm balmy night. She notices smoke coming from behind the shrub. She walks over to the source of the smoke

Shaun stands up, holding the cigarette behind his back

Shirley Hiya.
Shaun Shit. Don't creep up on people.
Shirley I wondered what you were doing.
Shaun Just getting some fresh air.
Shirley I can see that.
Shaun It gets so stuffy inside.
Shirley I saw the smoke and ——
Shaun (*displaying the cigarette*) Yeah, I'm smoking all right.
Shirley Fine by me.
Shaun The good thing is, though — no calories.
Shirley That's good, then.
Shaun Don't mention it, will you?
Shirley It's nothing to do with me.
Shaun The thing is, I'm in a non-smoking room. My dad phones up to see
if they can smell smoke in my room.
Shirley How do you know?
Shaun The first time I had one the housekeeper told me they were going to
put me in another room. That got back to him and he stopped my allowance.
Shirley It's a lovely place, isn't it?
Shaun I think it's a toilet.
Shirley Aren't you enjoying it?
Shaun It's a nightmare.
Shirley Why are you here, then?
Shaun Dad said I should come and get in shape for my degree. He must think
you have to pass a fitness test or something.
Shirley So he's paying for you to relax here before you take your exams?
Shaun Yeah, I've just said that.
Shirley Sorry.
Shaun God, some people.
Shirley If I thought my kids spoke to adults like you've just spoken to
me …
Shaun I'm not a kid.
Shirley Enjoy your cigarette.
Shaun Ken wants to play me at squash.
Shirley I'd like to watch that.
Shaun Why, do you think he'll win?
Shirley I don't really care.
Shaun It's a waste of time me taking my exams because I'm going to flunk
them anyway, just to spite him.
Shirley Sounds like you're really close.
Shaun Yeah, we are actually, OK? OK, Porky!
Shirley You know what the sad thing is? It's people like you who'll be
running this country in the next twenty years.

Shaun With any luck. Where are you from?
Shirley Buxton.
Shaun Where's that?
Shirley North Derbyshire. Where are you from?
Shaun Windsor.
Shirley Where's that?
Shaun God, don't you know where Windsor is?
Shirley Well, good luck with your exams.
Shaun Yeah, well, I'm going to fail my exams and then kill myself.
Shirley Why don't you kill yourself anyway, save all that revising.
Shaun You think you're amusing. Well, you're not, you're just another middle-aged bozo who's trying to get their youth back.

Shaun exits US

Shirley follows Shaun US *but stops before the exit*

Shirley On seconds thoughts why don't I kill you?

Don enters. He is dirty and carries a small carrier bag secreted under his track suit. The bag contains Cornish pasties, crisps, a Mars bar and a bottle of wine

Shirley Where've you been? I thought you were in the flotation tank?
Don Yeah, I did that, then I went out on a bike.
Shirley Look at you.
Don I came off the sodding thing.
Shirley How did you manage that?
Don The chain came off.
Shirley It could only happen to you.
Don (*holding up the plastic carrier*) Look! Goodies. I am bloody ravenous. I've got three Cornish pasties and some crisps.
Shirley That's cheating.
Don I know.
Shirley And all the money we're paying?
Don Honestly, if I don't have some stodge I will hang myself. Oh, yeah, and for afters: a Mars bar. Work rest and especially play. Do you want any or not?
Shirley I've lost three pounds, though.
Don To eat or not to eat, that is the question? To eat to dream!
Shirley What sort are they?
Don Beefy.

Shirley Bring 'em over here.

Don and Shirley move to a secret area of the garden where they are more hidden

Don Brilliant!

Shirley Don't let anybody see us for God's sake, or we'll get detention.

Don Yeah, we'll have to do a hundred sit-ups and not be able to play out for a week.

Shirley Where are the pasties from?

Don A Shell garage. All the other shops were closed. We're in the middle of nowhere. The only person I saw had two heads. (*He devours a Cornish pasty during the following*) Heaven!

Shirley I don't like 'em when they're cold.

Don I'll have yours.

Shirley No chance.

Don Shall I go in and ask 'em to warm 'em up?

Shirley I don't think it's the thing to do.

Don (*with his mouth full*) Neither is this. Oh by the way, I owe you twenty quid.

Shirley Why?

Don Ken's a monk. He's never drunk in his life. And he told me what you said to him, by the way — I mean, what are you playing at?

Shirley It was only a joke.

Don Shirley, telling a stranger you want mindless sex is not a joke.

Shirley I just said it to see his reaction. It slipped out.

Don Honestly. It's like living with a pervert.

Shirley I do fancy that, you know?

Don Don't spoil the picnic; I risked my life for this.

Don and Shirley recline together. This is as close as they have been during their week

Shirley What does this remind you of?

Don Bamburgh.

Shirley We never go any more.

Don It's time, isn't it?

Shirley Do you know what I like most about picnics?

Don There's no washing-up?

Shirley Apart from that. Cheese and tomato sandwiches. And coffee from the flask. I love that. I think it's because you've wrapped 'em all up — makes it more special, you know, like some hidden treasure?

Don And cheese and onion crisps; they always taste better on a picnic.

Shirley Can you remember when we got attacked by that sheep?
Don It wasn't a sheep, it was a goat. A big 'un and all.
Shirley And me and the kids got in the car and locked you out.
Don Yeah, I've still got a bruise somewhere.
Shirley We've had some good laughs.
Don You know, when we get back, I think we should employ a masseuse.
Shirley Good idea.
Don We can have a loft conversion and she can live in the attic. Every morning we can have Equilibrium or a Full Body.
Shirley Yes, please. (*Indicating the pasty*) This is nice.
Don We can ask if they'd rent Chloë out to us.
Shirley (*with a full mouth*) Yeah, I'm sure I'd lose weight if somebody came to call for me every morning.
Don Depends who it was.

A beat

Shirley (*chewing*) Do you still find me attractive, Don?
Don Eh?
Shirley Do you still find me attractive?
Don Yeah.
Shirley You liar.
Don I do.
Shirley But … ?
Don Have you rung home?
Shirley Yes, Sam's fine, and Holly's got a guitar lesson. Your mum says she hates the teacher.
Don My mum hates everybody.
Shirley Holly, you drip.
Don I know.
Shirley Do you miss 'em, when it's just me and you?
Don No.
Shirley You do.
Don I have this vision of their hearts beating. You know, like when we saw them before they were born. It's really stayed with me, has that. I just have this image of their little hearts pumping. I keep hoping that they won't stop.
Shirley What goes on in your head?
Don Don't you think that?
Shirley No, I've never even thought about it before.
Don I couldn't bear anything happening to them. Shit!
Shirley What wrong?

Don pulls a bottle of wine from the plastic bag

Don Nearly forgot.
Shirley You don't need that.
Don Oh yes I do.

Don tries to open the bottle during the following

Shirley Push the cork in.
Don I'm trying to. Bollocks. This is a disaster. We can't have a midnight feast
    without this.
Shirley Nip to the car, there's a bottle opener.
Don No there isn't , I threw it out. We can't have a picnic without a drink.
    This is my birthday party.
Shirley Your birthday's tomorrow.
Don Tomorrow's an off alcohol day.
Shirley There's one on the Swiss Army knife in the first aid kit.

Don stands and moves to the exit

Don I love the Swiss; a brilliant race, so resourceful.

Don exits

*Shirley checks that Don is completely out of the way and then attacks another
pasty*

Gertrude enters and moves up behind Shirley

Shirley sees Gertrude and stuffs the pasty into her mouth

Gertrude Glorious night.
Shirley Mmmm.
Gertrude Wondered why you were out here. Glorious.
Shirley Mmmhmmhmm.
Gertrude Toothache?
Shirley Mmmm.
Gertrude Try cloves, love; works for me every time. I still have most of my
    bottom set, you know?
Shirley Mmmm!
Gertrude Are you nibbling?
Shirley Nnnnnoo.
Gertrude That's very naughty of you, love.

Silence

Shirley (*holding out a bag of crisps to Gertrude*) Crisp?
Gertrude What flavour are they?
Shirley Beef.
Gertrude Oh beefy, my favourite, don't mind if I do. (*She takes a crisp*)
Shirley Have the bag; I've got some more.

Shirley gets another bag of crisps

Gertrude (*getting comfortable*) Oh well, "Hail to thee blithe spirit."
Shirley Coward?
Gertrude Shelley, love, Shelley. The exuberance of life. Well, this is rather nice, isn't it? A veritable *Midsummer Night's Dream*, dear.

A moment

I used to sit in a garden like this and read for hours. Do you know Shakespeare?
Shirley I did.
Gertrude I have those tapes, you know — Derek Jacobi ...
Shirley I wanted to act.
Gertrude Good grief, really?
Shirley Never really got very far.
Gertrude Did you ever meet J.B. Priestley?
Shirley No, but I sat behind Ian McKellen once.
Gertrude I thought he was a lovely writer. And Bernard Shaw.
Shirley I did some acting at university. And then I toured with a community group.
Gertrude Never fancied it myself. Living out of a suitcase, most of the time, aren't they? Fancied the law if anything. Never had any application really.
Shirley It was something that I'd always wanted to do.
Gertrude I saw the Three Tenors; have you seen them?
Shirley Yes.
Gertrude Oh, good, whereabouts?
Shirley We've got the video.
Gertrude Yes, I saw them at the first one. And then I saw the big one in London.
Shirley Pavarotti.
Gertrude I love opera — do you love opera? Nice and beefy, aren't they?
Shirley The Three Tenors?
Gertrude The crisps, dear.

A beat

Shirley So I gave it up after a while.

Gertrude The acting?

Shirley Gave it up.

Gertrude Why would you do that? Sounds like a silly thing to do if you liked doing it.

Shirley I married Don.

Gertrude Was it a mistake, dear?

Shirley Well ... ?

Gertrude He's a plumber, isn't he? That can be very useful. Does he make a living out of it?

Shirley Well, he designs and fits.

Gertrude Oh, well, that sounds wonderful, really.

Shirley But I think it's still inside me.

Gertrude The acting? Of course it is, love. You never let go of the things you really want to do.

Shirley It's too late now. I'm in an amateur group.

Gertrude Nonsense. It's never too late. I went to Africa the year before last, on a safari.

Shirley Really?

Gertrude And I rode in the jeep, rifle on my lap, love — wonderful. Seventy-two and I thought "Dash this, I've done everything else", so I thought I'd give it a go. I may do a bungee jump for my birthday.

Shirley I don't like heights.

Gertrude Thinking about it, probably won't — but you never know. Probably settle for a facial, but ...

Shirley What did you do?

Gertrude In the real world? This and that, love. Helped in the village mostly, that kind of thing. Organized fêtes, money-raising for the Hospice. Do you know St Martin's — lovely place?

Shirley Oh, I thought you may have been in business.

Gertrude No, no need, really. Stayed at home most of the time. Helped out really — didn't have to work, which is a bit of a bind in itself. And then when I married Lawrence he took good care of me. He was a publisher. Look, do you mind awfully if I smoke?

Shirley No ... I ...

Gertrude Since we're being naughty. It's just the odd cigar, love. And is there anything else on the alfresco menu this evening?

Shirley There's a pasty from the Shell garage.

Gertrude Oh, no, I think I'll pass on that, love. If you don't mind, go straight into the cheese and biscuits.

A beat

Shirley So doesn't your husband come?

Gertrude He died.
Shirley Oh, I am sorry.
Gertrude So am I dear. Ten years ago. So — I spend most of my time pottering. May as well, love, no-one to speak to at home any more. Stop here, get bored, go to Champney's. Have you been?
Shirley No, we go to Centre Parcs, though.
Gertrude You'd love it. Then come back, go on a cruise, do my bungee, help in the village ...
Shirley We don't get away much really.
Gertrude It really is life in the fast lane.
Shirley What did he die from?
Gertrude Amputation it was, love. Suffered for years with it, wouldn't have it seen to. Too busy with work and one thing and another. Went in for a leg off, and got a blood clot and that was it. So sudden, completely out of the blue. Never did anyone any harm, love, and then he's gone, like a puff of smoke. Quite horrible really. Look after them, love; you never miss them, really, till they're gone.

Ken enters, wearing a jogging suit. He is full of beans

Ken Midnight feast?
Gertrude Do join us, Ben. It's not the Waldorf, darling, but I'm rather enjoying it. Crisp, Ben? Beefy. Only two hundred calories a bag.
Shirley There'll be some wine in a minute; Don's just gone for the opener.
Ken Yeah, I've seen him; what's he been doing?
Shirley He fell off a bike.
Ken Brown's not one of his colours either, is it?
Shirley What have you been telling my husband, anyway? I'm going to have to learn to keep my mouth shut.
Ken If I wasn't a gentleman ...
Gertrude You out jogging, Ben?
Ken Had a little bit of good news today, so I'm treating myself to an extra run.
Gertrude That's a perverse way of celebrating, love. You must be so fit it's sickening.
Ken Well ...
Gertrude I wish I was, I really do; there's so much I still want to do.
Ken Yes, I've landed myself a prime cul-de-sac plot in York that they're going to let me develop.
Gertrude Congratulations, love.
Ken Six figures. What is it they say? "That'll do nicely."
Gertrude Oh, well done.
Ken Yes, just what the doctor ordered.

Shirley So how much are you worth now?
Ken Ah ah.
Gertrude He won't tell us.
Ken I thought it was impolite to ask.
Shirley I bet he's a millionaire.
Gertrude Oh really, I do hope so.
Shirley I've never been this close to a real millionaire before.
Ken It's a nice development about a hundred yards from the river. Six houses, three hundred thousand each.
Gertrude It is worth all the effort, though, Ben?
Ken Well the thing is it's money in the bank. I mean, with respect, you've got the accent and all that, but have you got the money in the bank? That's what it's about at the end of the day.
Gertrude I've never really had any dealings with money.
Ken So you've no idea how it feels then.
Gertrude Lawrence was like you, darling. Worked hard, love. Wasn't quite as good at squash, I dare say, but used aftershave with rather more discretion.
Ken That's the trouble with you lot. There's a lot of talk and no proof. How much hard cash can you lay your hands on then? A couple of hundred grand? I've got that in my current account.
Shirley Ken?
Ken How much are you worth then? I'll tell you what I'm worth. One point five, and that's without this new development. One point five.

Gertrude stands and makes to leave

Shirley You can't take it with you though, can you?
Ken I don't want to take it with me.
Gertrude I think I shall have a walk around the grounds.
Ken So how much are we talking then?
Gertrude Ben, you shouldn't ask, you know.
Ken Yeah, but is it millions? This is what I want to know!
Gertrude I think it's hundreds of millions, really; do you know I've really no idea. I don't really deal with actual cash, you know. Anyway, thanks for the picnic. I must say I feel rather naughty now. A walk around the garden should get me a burn, shouldn't it?
Shirley Oh yes.
Gertrude Good grief, Ben, you've gone quite pale!

Gertrude drifts off stage

Ken and Shirley are silent together

Shirley So there ... !
Ken I've been thinking about what you said.
Shirley Oh listen, I ... erm ...
Ken I mean, if you're ever up in the Dales ...
Shirley I shouldn't have said anything.
Ken I'll leave you my card if ——
Shirley Better not.
Ken I mean, if ever you're looking for something completely mindless.
Shirley No, honestly ... Ben, Ken, erm ...
Ken Just a thought.
Shirley No, really.
Ken I mean if he's not ——
Shirley Look, I'm ——
Ken I think I've got what you need.
Shirley Ken? Well, thanks for the offer, anyway.

Ken walks US *and exits*

As Ken goes, Shirley looks at the Mars bar. She cannot resist it, and she starts to eat it. She is in ecstasy as she devours the chocolate bar

Don arrives with the bottle opener, equally ecstatic. He immediately picks up the bottle of wine

Don You OK? You look a bit flushed.
Shirley Oh yeah, I'm fine. Gertrude's been for a nibble. She's loaded apparently.
Don Did you get her phone number? (*He opens the bottle*) And finally ... (*He drinks*)
Shirley Don't overdo it.
Don Oh yes! I needed that.
Shirley Give us it here.

Don gives Shirley the bottle and she drinks. Don reclines and takes the bottle back

Don Now this is more like it. It's like the Summer Ball of 1978.
Shirley Don't guzzle it.
Don You can have all the money in the world, but ...
Shirley Do you feel better?
Don I do now.
Shirley Chilling out?
Don Well I had a flutter in my chest on the bike. I think it was the fear of being caught.

A beat

(*Looking in the plastic bag*) Where's the other bag of crisps gone?
Shirley I gave them to Gertrude.
Don Why?
Shirley I just did.
Don Couldn't she afford any of her own?
Shirley I don't think she deals with cash.
Don I can't believe you've given my crisps away. I'm absolutely starving.
I'm a stick insect and you've given them away. I'm surprised there's any
pasties left.
Shirley Come here and kiss us.
Don Why?
Shirley Because it's romantic.

Shirley attempts to grab Don

Don No, don't. I'm not in the mood.
Shirley What, because somebody's ate your crisps?

Don kisses Shirley. It is an innocent and short-lived kiss

Don There you go.
Shirley No, a proper kiss.
Don That was a proper kiss.
Shirley Just try.
Don Well, what do you want me to do, ravish you in the bushes, like I used
to? I told you not to read that book. It's rotting your brain. We've gone
beyond sex, didn't you know that?
Shirley Have we?
Don I think we have.
Shirley Come on, touch my leg.
Don What for?
Shirley Because it's nice.

Don touches her leg without feeling

Don There, how's that?
Shirley Oh, Don.
Don I'm not, you know.
Shirley Shall I touch you?
Don Please, Shirl, no.
Shirley I don't know why I bother.

Don Just leave it.
Shirley Come on, you've had a drink, haven't you?
Don Oh, funny.
Shirley Just try.
Don No.
Shirley Why?
Don Because it's so false.
Shirley It's you who's false, you've always put on an act.
Don Oh, listen who's talking, last season's Virginia Woolf. (*He has another swig of wine*)
Shirley Look at you.
Don I'm only having a wet.
Shirley Just try and touch me again.
Don Why?
Shirley I want you to.
Don No, OK, no, I don't feel like it. It don't feel like touching Ginger Spice's bloody legs, all right?

A beat

Shirley I thought we were doing too well. I thought we were actually communicating on an even keel. (*She stands and makes to leave. She takes the plastic bag with her*)
Don Where're you going?
Shirley I'm going to bed.
Don What for?
Shirley Because I'm tired.
Don I thought we were supposed to be having a picnic!
Shirley Grow up!
Don Going to read your book, are you?
Shirley No, I'm going to Ken's; he's got what I need, apparently.
Don I wouldn't be surprised.
Shirley What would you do if I did? Cry? Sorry. I didn't mean that.
Don It wouldn't be the first time you've done that on me. Don't worry I can remember you at college.
Shirley Oh, we've had a drink, have we?
Don Yes, we have, thank God.
Shirley You're pathetic.
Don At least I'm not ashamed of my past.
Shirley What past? You never had one.
Don I did.
Shirley And I'm not ashamed of mine.
Don I can see the way Holly's going.

Shirley Well, I hope to God Sam's not like you, poor sod.

Don I was a sex machine at college.

Shirley Well, you're not even a washing machine now, are you?

Don Where's the Mars bar gone?

Shirley I've eaten it.

Don We were going to share that.

Shirley Well, tough titties, I've eaten it and it was bloody wonderful.

Don Well, throw us my pasty then!

Shirley takes the remaining pasty and throws it into some bushes or into some water

Shirley Here. I hope it chokes you. I'm sick of it, sick of you and your bloody panic attacks, and your pains and funny feelings. Talk about stress: your anxieties are bloody killing me. You spoil everything, you always have.

Shirley departs

Don stands and has a big swig of wine. He sits. He shouts after Shirley, then begins to cry

Don (*crying*) Shirley? Shirley? Shirley?

Music plays: Puccini's Humming Chorus

   Don slowly exits

Black-out

SCENE 3

The hall area

The next morning

There is a sun lounger on stage

The music fades

Ken enters. He is preparing to go for a jog

Shaun enters from the opposite side of the stage and crosses towards Ken. He has just returned from the squash courts

Shaun I've just beaten the squash coach two-one. He didn't know where to put himself. In fact I'm working my way through all the residents.

Ken So you fancy your chances?

Shaun Well, age is on my side.

Ken You'd better book a court then.

Shaun We could do it now, if you want.

Ken I'm going for a run now, then I've got a court booked and after that I'm having a full body massage.

Shaun You have one every day, don't you?

Ken Yeah, I know!

Shaun Whatever turns you on.

Ken Exactly.

Shaun So are we on, then?

Ken Tomorrow morning, early, I'll give you a thrashing before I have my feet done. Book a court.

Shaun How early?

Ken Very early.

Ken walks off, about to start his jog

Zoë enters

Shaun (*moving to the exit*) I've just beaten the squash coach two-one. So what about that, then?

Zoë I beat him three-nil yesterday, so I wouldn't get too excited about it.

Shaun Two-one, though! Excellent!

Shirley enters. She has a large box with her

Zoë Didn't see you at Aqua Tone today.

Shirley No, I've been working on something in the art room I wanted to finish. Besides I feel like one of the Woodentops.

Zoë Oh, dear.

Shirley I'm walking like Spotty Dog at the moment.

Zoë Tell me about it.

Shirley Don't your legs ache?

Zoë They kill me! The thing is you've got to keep going because there's always somebody younger coming up behind.

Shirley You're not here permanently?

Zoë No way, if I damage my ankle or I can't deliver I'm out of a job. Where's Don?

Shirley He went to the chiropractor. It was the only treatment that was free. Said he wanted to go and try it.

Zoë Didn't he know that the chiropractor is a judo expert?

Shirley Rough, is he?

Zoë I think the phrase is "firm".

Shirley He'll be all right, he's quite tough really.
Zoë He scared me to death on Monday. I thought we'd lost him.
Shirley No, I'm not that lucky. It was a joke; don't look so serious.
Zoë I thought you meant it.

Don enters. He feels a little worse for wear because of the drink and is walking very tall because of his dealings with the chiropractor

Don What a bloody nightmare.
Shirley What's wrong now?
Don I think he was trying to break my neck. He's got a towel under my chin, a foot on the back of my head and he's pulling me backwards with all of his weight. He's about seventeen stone and all. I couldn't get out of the door when he'd finished. I bet I'm three inches taller.
Shirley (*under her breath*) Pity that he can't do that with all your bits.
Don I bet I don't fit in the bloody car. Look at me, I'm a giant.
Zoë Seventies Dance tonight Don — are you into it?
Don Dunno, I'll have to see how it goes. If I feel this tall, I might go and pick some bananas instead.
Zoë Make you feel mighty real.
Don I thought I was having Chloë.
Zoë It's just basic dance steps.
Don How come I'm not convinced?
Zoë You'll love it; you can bop till you drop.
Shirley Literally.
Zoë Right, I'd better go see how many I'm having.

Zoë exits

Shirley Headache gone?
Don It had until he got his hands on me.
Shirley He does judo, apparently.
Don I knew he did something when he started to stick my leg up my arse!
Shirley Why did you go to the chiropractor, there's nothing wrong with your back.
Don There is now.

A beat

Sorry about last night.
Shirley Yeah, well.
Don Sorry.
Shirley At least you tried.

Don I like just crushing up and going to sleep best, don't you?
Shirley Yeah, of course I do.

A beat

Don What's in the box?
Shirley My artwork. I couldn't be bothered to take it up.
Don Can I have a look?
Shirley No, you'll only criticize it.
Don I won't.
Shirley Leave it.
Don Go on, let's have a look. What is it?
Shirley A sculpture.
Don Can I open it?
Shirley No.

Don picks up the box, places it on the sun lounger and takes Shirley's sculpture out of it. The sculpture is of an enormous tree stump with accompanying shrubs; however it could be misconstrued as being a large phallus

Don What is it?
Shirley Eh?
Don What's it supposed to be?
Shirley It's a sculpture.
Don What of?
Shirley I call it "Tree of Life".
Don "Tree of Life"?
Shirley Jan, the teacher, thinks it's quite good.
Don It is.
Shirley It's a tree with flora.
Don Right.
Shirley Jan says it's one of those pieces that can be whatever you want to see.
    He says I've cleverly caught the ambivalence and paradox in art. I suppose
    it's really a piece about freedom.
Don What sort of freedom?
Shirley Don't you think it's beautiful? Be honest.
Don Well, if I'm being honest I think it's a bit disturbing.
Shirley There is something liberating about it.
Don My heart's racing just picking the thing up.
Shirley Don't break it.
Don What are you going to do with it?
Shirley I thought your mum might like it.

Don Where would she put it?

Shirley Jan says it's in the eye of the beholder.

Don I mean I'm not a prude, Shirl, but pornographic literature and now this ...

Shirley Meaning?

Don Well, it's something deeply personal, isn't it?

Shirley I knew you'd misunderstand it.

Don Hey, don't take it out on me.

Shirley You always put me down, no matter what I do.

Don Wow, steady on.

Shirley Even at college you did it.

Don A little bit of criticism, that's all.

Shirley I was never good enough. "You weren't very good in that, I couldn't hear you at the back". "Get back down Shirley Weston, back into your shell, woman, where you belong." "You, do anything vaguely interesting, get away?" Even if I've got a migraine you always have to have one worse. If I get a cold, you've got hypothermia. As if you're Mr Perfect. It might come as a shock to you, Don, but you're not perfect.

Don I know that; I saw myself in the mirror last night.

Shirley In fact, far from it.

Don I know that, and you're not thin.

Shirley Well, I am not fat.

Don No, and you're not a thin person, are you?

Shirley So are you saying you think I'm fat?

Don I'm not saying you're fat.

Shirley So what are you saying?

Don Well, you're not a stick.

Shirley And I'm not a blob.

Don And you're not a stick.

Shirley So what are you saying?

Don You're not thin, let's be honest.

Shirley How can you say I'm fat? Your mother's fat. I am not fat.

Don Well ... ?

Shirley What about you? When you'd been playing squash you looked like a tomato.

Don Oh, bring that up.

Shirley And you didn't even score a point. Talk about embarassing.

Don I knew you fancied that Ken. Just your type, isn't he?

Shirley Didn't even score a point.

Don Yeah, yeah, that's me, I'm a mouse aren't I? Nothing but a bloody mouse. At least I haven't got a fat stomach and fat legs.

Shirley You what?

Don You heard.

Silence

Shirley Right.
Don Sorry.
Shirley Right.
Don Sorry. I didn't mean to say that.
Shirley I will never forgive you for that.
Don Shirl. I'm sorry.
Shirley You know I've got a thing about that.
Don Well, since we're telling the truth.

Ken enters. He has just been for a jog

Ken Wow, not bad, two miles in just over ten minutes. All right then, how's the birthday boy? (*He notices the sculpture*) Oh, that looks interesting!
Shirley Before you say anything, it's supposed to be a tree.
Ken Looks like a prick to me.
Don Yeah, well, it's a tree, all right?
Shirley I made it earlier.
Ken You couldn't make me one like it, could you? What's it called, "Memories"? What are you going to do with it?
Don I could guess.
Ken It's good, isn't it?
Shirley Oh, honestly.
Ken Don't fancy another game of squash, do you? You want to come and watch, Shirley — he might actually score a point.
Shirley No, I hate motorway accidents.
Ken Tell you what, we could play for a few quid if you want?
Don Never been my game, squash, really. I played in the third fifteen at university.
Ken A rugger bugger eh?
Don I played a bit.
Ken You know what they say?
Don Actually, Ken, it's a man's game, mate.
Ken And squash isn't?
Don Well, let's be honest ...
Ken What are you saying, mate?
Don Forget it?
Ken You don't fancy your chances, do you?
Don I'm not a violent man, Ken, thankfully.
Ken Well, it's a good job, isn't it?
Don Actually it is.
Ken Oh, right.

Don I mean, I could lose my rag over what you said to Shirl.

Ken I only bought her a bloody flapjack, what's your problem? And I wouldn't recommend it.

Shirley Neither would I.

Ken I mean, I've been doing Aikido for five years, mate, so unless your stomach throws are up to scratch I'd give it a body swerve.

Don Yeah, well, maybe I will. I did a bit of karate at college.

Ken Oh right?

Don Yeah, yeah.

Ken Well, I'd better go and thrash some poor sod at squash.

Shirley Yeah, I think you'd better.

Ken See you around, and if you fancy twenty minutes on the mat, Don, just give me a shout.

Ken laughs and exits

Don sits

Shirley When did you do any karate?

Don University.

Shirley You went to one lesson, and you gave it up because it hurt your knuckles. (*She moves* US *as if to exit*)

Don Where are you going?

Shirley I've got reflexology in ten minutes.

Don I'm ready for off, are you?

Shirley Well, I can't say it's been relaxing. You've got to let go, Don.

Don I do try.

Shirley Anyway. (*She makes another move to go*)

Don I do love you.

Shirley Do you?

Don I do, I'm not just feeling myself.

Shirley Well you're not feeling me either, are you?

Don Oh, don't joke.

Shirley Don, I've got to, love. I've got to laugh and joke or I'd bloody cry, I would, honest. How did we ever get like this, honestly?

A beat

Don We'll get it sorted.

Shirley Just don't tell me how you feel every five minutes; that might help.

Don There isn't another woman.

Shirley There's no bloody wonder, is there?

Don I thought you'd think that there was.

Shirley It had crossed my mind.
Don I'd never do that to you.
Shirley No, right.
Don Would you do that to me? You don't have to answer that.
Shirley I can't understand you. You, you seem to have stopped living. I mean you're frozen in time. The way things are going, Don, you may as well be dead, or pickled or something.
Don Oh, come on.
Shirley It's not just the sex, it's bloody everything.

A beat

Don Can you remember us at college?
Shirley We were different people.
Don We did all sorts.
Shirley He was a sexy bloke then, was Don Weston, can you remember?

Shirley moves further US *without her sculpture*

Don Hey?
Shirley What?
Don You've forgotten your penis thing.
Shirley Which one?

Shirley exits. Don follows her off, sheepishly carrying the sculpture

Music plays and the Lights fade

SCENE 4

Aerobics Studio

The music from the previous scene fades. It is now evening in the Aerobics Studio

Gertrude strolls on

Zoë enters

Zoë It's Seventies Dance in here, Mrs Tate.
Gertrude I like to watch, lovey.
Zoë They're waiting for you in the treatment area.
Gertrude Not tonight, love, I absolutely ache. I'm almost blue with bruising, darling.

Zoë Can they let your Multi-Method go, then?

Gertrude Yes, dear, yes, of course, let it all go.

Zoë It will be charged to your account I'm afraid.

Gertrude Then charge it, dear, I really don't care. I'm bored with the silly thing, anyway. One of the girls has fingernails on her like a razor, quite dreadful work, honestly.

Zoë I'll go and tell them to let the treatment go, then.

Zoë exits US

Don enters

Gertrude My word, love. Are you dancing?

Don In for a penny.

Gertrude Jolly good. I like to watch.

Don So do I, usually.

Gertrude Back tomorrow, aren't you? Just getting nicely settled and it's time to go.

Don Do you mind if I ask you something?

Gertrude Is it personal? Never really been into the personal side of things. A failing really.

Don What do you think when you look back?

Gertrude I never look back, love. Memories, yes, very important, darling. I can remember my mother having a photo taken with an ostrich. It only had one leg, dear.

Don Oh, right.

Gertrude Eyesight's not what it was, though. I wish I was going deaf and not blind. And I love music. Do you?

Don Puccini.

Gertrude Simply the best.

Don Tina Turner.

Gertrude But I can't stand the thought of darkness.

Don So what is there to look forward to?

Gertrude The porn channel, love. I was joking, darling. Oh, you are a morbid morsel, aren't you?

Don Don't you fear death?

Gertrude There isn't a lot I can do about that. The worse parts of living are like dying, love; you have to do it all by yourself. Now, why are you thinking like this? You've got another thirty years ahead of you. It's an entire life. So what is there to worry about?

Don I feel guilty about being here.

Gertrude One does, love, but what can one do?

Don Not come?

Gertrude Now don't be silly, darling, that's just silly.

Don You should be able to get all this stuff on the National Health!

Gertrude Yes, I agree. But, I mean, can you imagine what it would be like here, darling? One wouldn't be able to move for ankle chains. Listen, life is unfair, love. That's the whole game. You have to know that and just get on with it. Nobody owes you a living.

Don Yes, but — you can do what you want. I've never done what I've wanted. I mean I never really wanted to go to university, to be honest. I never wanted to get married.

Gertrude Oh, dear!

Don I didn't want to have children, really, not deep down.

Gertrude Couldn't bear that love, unnatural somehow.

Don I fancied a life of debauchery, young girls, poetry and beer.

Gertrude Yes, that sounds quite wonderful.

Don I mean tomorrow's the future, and I'll still be fitting bloody kitchens! And then suddenly I'm at the Pearly Gates, and I sum up my life by telling St Peter that I could do him a nice twin sink bowl with marble effect and a secreted swing bin, at no extra cost!

Gertrude Sounds like a change, dear.

Don I need some space.

Gertrude Then you should get out, love.

Don I need time on my own.

Gertrude It's better for the both of you. Just go, love. Forty years ahead of you. A whole new life. Wouldn't it be absolutely wonderful, darling?

Don Yes!

Gertrude We should all have life in two halves, love. Forty years. Draw a line underneath it, and start again with someone else. Think of it. It would be like having two lives, and all the things you did wrong you could decide whether or not to do wrong again. Life's always chasing its own tail. Just go. A note and gone, love!

Don That's right.

Gertrude Forty more years of bickering, of children, of the blessed in-laws, love.

Don Absolutely.

Gertrude I've seen what it does. Business, family, working for nothing, a few pounds and saving up for a chalet holiday; is that really what you want, for the rest of your life? Larkin, darling: "Get out as early as you can."

Don Good old Philip.

Gertrude Be unreasonable, love.

Don I don't know.

Gertrude You're not a coward, are you?

Shirley enters US. *She is dressed for the dance class*

Shirley Hiya!
Don Hiya!

Zoë returns with her cassette player. Ken comes in also

Zoë Right, Seventies Dance; you ready?
Ken I'm not dancing with him.
Gertrude Very good, Ben.
Zoë It's OK, Ken, you can dance with me.
Ken That's more like it.
Zoë And take it steady, Don; don't dance yourself dizzy.

Zoë switches on the cassette player and a dance track plays: "Disco Inferno". She moves DS and begins the routine. Gertrude taps her stick; Ken and Shirley move; Don stays still

Let's get going. Nice and easy to start with.

Ken and Shirley follow the instructions

Nice and easy: step, and clap. And a spin. Come on, Don.
Don Oh, I love this.
Gertrude Could you possibly turn it down a little? Yes, it's a nice beat, isn't it? But it's not Puccini is it?

Don begins to dance. But he does not dance in the aerobic fashion — it is his own free-form disco dance. He sings loudly to the music and walks over to Ken in a bizarre mixture of threat and comedy

Ken, Shirley and Zoë stop doing the class. They, and Gertrude, watch Don dance

Don sings out loudly and dances provocatively up to Zoë

   Shirley exits

Finally Zoë turns off the cassette

Don stands in silence, breathing heavily

Don Oh, spoil-sport, I was just getting into that!

Black-out

SCENE 5

Outside the Hall

It is the next morning. The atmosphere is fresh

Shirley enters, wearing her track suit. She is looking for Don

Shirley Don? (*She walks across the stage, calling down the gardens*) Don? (*She turns to move* US)

Gertrude enters with a number of pieces of golf equipment

Shirley Morning.
Gertrude Morning, dear.
Shirley You haven't seen Don, have you?
Gertrude Who, love?
Shirley Don.
Gertrude Ron?
Shirley Don!
Gertrude I've not seen a soul this morning.
Shirley I thought he might have gone for a run or ... erm ...? I've been down to the pool and he hasn't been down there, and he didn't have any treatments booked. I mean, we were supposed to be out of our rooms by ten.
Gertrude Oh.
Shirley So. I don't know what ...
Gertrude Oh.
Shirley What's wrong?
Gertrude Oh, well.
Shirley What?
Gertrude He's done it then.
Shirley Done what?
Gertrude Yes, we had a chat last night. He told me that he wanted some space, love.
Shirley Space?
Gertrude I must say, he wasn't entirely himself, love.
Shirley Well, I know he's a bit ——
Gertrude I'm afraid I told him that if he felt like that, then he should go.
Shirley Go ...
Gertrude Well, yes, darling, it's the only thing to do.
Shirley Leave the Hall, you mean?
Gertrude No. Leave you, dear!

Shirley Eh?

Gertrude You're killing each other, dear.

Shirley No ...

Gertrude I've seen it a hundred times. It's for the best, believe me.

Shirley No, we've always argued.

Gertrude He's gone, love, you should rejoice! I thought he was a coward, love, but he isn't. Which is something to be grateful for, I suppose.

Shirley But we've known each other for twenty-two years ...

Gertrude Oh, darling, be honest.

Shirley I've never known life without him.

Gertrude But what sort of life was it? A chalet in Bournemouth, love. It's like being buried alive.

Shirley Well, you get used to it ...

Gertrude From what I saw you weren't suited. It's a chance for you to start again, love.

Shirley Gone where, though?

Gertrude Into the nether, into the night. They always do. Here one minute and then ——

Shirley But what ... ?

Gertrude Time to start again, dear. Time to start acting: "O, for a muse of fire", love! Do the things you've always wanted to!

Shirley We can't afford that ...

Gertrude He had the thought in his head already, dear. He was stood on the edge of the cliff; all I did was hold his coat, love.

Shirley I'll go see if he's rung home.

Gertrude He won't. They never do. Just thank God he had the guts.

Shirley is distraught. She exits into the house

Gertrude stands alone

Gone, love, all gone. Wonderful gesture. A wonderful re-birth, love!

Don enters, fresh-faced from a massive walk

Don Morning!

Gertrude Morning, love, morning.

Don It's a bit fresher now ...

Gertrude You?

Don Me.

Gertrude I thought you'd gone to a better life?

Don No, I've been down to the market. Get something for tea. My mum'll have forgotten to get anything.

Gertrude It was all sound advice, darling.

Don It might have been for you. But I've got kids. I've got a family. I've got people who still love me.

Gertrude I know, love, that's why you should go.

Don I've got a life to live, though. You ought to get out there; there's a bloody world out there, you know! Buy yourself some broccoli. Live a bit. There's going to be some changes in my life, anyway.

Gertrude You've just missed the biggest one.

Don I won't miss the next one. We're going to get a caravan. A nice five berth.

Gertrude Oh, hell on earth, love.

Don Shirley says we don't take enough breaks. So ——

Gertrude How absolutely awful!!

Don There's some great sites up north-east. Ireland. I've never been.

Gertrude In a caravan … ?

Don I'm going to make the next forty years count.

Gertrude You need serious psychiatric help, love. You should book yourself into a clinic immediately.

Don I'm not going to be forty again, I'll tell you that.

Gertrude You are quite insane, darling.

Gertrude hobbles off DL

Don heads towards the exit to the Hall

Shirley enters from the Hall, very distraught

Don stops

Shirley Where've you been? I have been worried to death about you. Don't disappear like that. I don't know if you've had a heart attack, gone native or what?

Don Wow, steady.

Shirley My bloody nerves are shattered with you!

Don Calm down.

Shirley I've phoned home, your mum's worried now, so are the kids … I've got a tightness in my chest.

Don Listen, I was telling Gertrude: I think we should get a caravan.

Shirley What?

Don A nice little second-hand tourer.

Shirley Two thousand pounds we've just spent, and you want to buy a caravan?

Don And an awning for a barbecue, the kids'll love that!

Shirley You hate the outdoor life!
Don And I'm going to grow my hair!
Shirley What for?
Don And treat myself to one of them biker's jackets!
Shirley You haven't even got a bike.
Don We can go down to Cornwall. And I'll take you to a disco!
Shirley They don't have over-forties' nights!
Don Just think of the sound of the rain on the roof.
Shirley How are we going to make love in a caravan?
Don We can get a metal detector.
Shirley We are not getting a caravan. They're for old people.
Don We are old people.
Shirley You are. Think what Maxine and Thomas would say if we bought
a caravan?
Don We're getting one.
Shirley We're not, no, it's not us. We're better than that!

Don becomes very emotional; this gives way to tears during the following

Don No, we're not, that's the point; we're not better than that. We're getting
one. I never do what I want. I have never done what I've wanted in forty
years. I have always got to compromize ... Well, no. No, no. no! Sod you,
sod the kids, sod my mother's knicker elastic, and Thomas who doesn't
need a drink, sod squash, sod slide, sod the fitted kitchens and the panic
attacks. Sod it, sod it! We're changing, all right? We're starting again! All
right? All right?

Shirley holds Don as he weeps

Shirley Where are we going to keep a bloody caravan?
Don Oh God, I'm sorry.
Shirley It's OK.
Don I want to run away, Shirl.
Shirley I know you do.
Don I did try. I did try, but I'm such a coward.
Shirley No, you're not a coward.
Don Hold me, Shirl.
Shirley Where's your Shirl?
Don Kiss me ...

*Shirley kisses Don on the lips. He weeps. He is in a state of complete stress;
a breakdown*

Don Oh God, love! I can't stand it ...

Shirley Don't call me love, all right?
Don Can I call you blob?
Shirley Yes, but don't call me love.
Don Oh, hell.
Shirley (*nursing him*) So have you enjoyed it then?
Don (*crying*) Yeah. Have you?
Shirley Oh yeah, it's been relaxing and I've lost two pounds.
Don I've not lost anything.
Shirley Oh, I think you have.

Don is completely wracked with tears. But then the tears become laughter

Shirley hugs Don

Don A caravan, I must be going crackers!

Don laughs and hugs Shirley

There is a look of horror on Shirley's face. She weeps US *of Don, unseen by him but not by the audience*

Delibes' "Flower Duet" plays

The Lights slowly fade

The CURTAIN *slowly falls*

FURNITURE AND PROPERTY LIST

ACT I
SCENE 1

On stage: Cupboard. *In it*: Reebok slide equipment: mats and covers for trainers
                    Step equipment
                    Sports bags
                    Portable cassette player

Personal: **Don**: itinerary
                    Shirley: itinerary

During lighting change p. 6

Set: Wicker chair

SCENE 2

Off stage: Massage table with towels, bottles of oil etc. (**Chloë**)

SCENE 3

Off stage: Chairs, table (**Bellboy**)
                    Hanging baskets (**Stage Management**)
                    Cup of tea (**Ken**)
                    Bag containing small booklet, mug of coffee (**Shirley**)
                    Newspaper (**Gertrude**)

Personal: **Gertrude**: stick (used throughout)

SCENE 4

Strike: Hanging baskets
                    Seating except wicker chair

Set: Cassette player

Off stage: Glass of water (**Zoë**)

Personal: **Don**: heart rate monitor

SCENE 5

Off stage: Massage table (**Chloë**)

SCENE 6

Off stage: Drip on wheels (**Maggie**)
Squash racket (**Ken**)

ACT II

SCENE 1

Set: Squash rackets for **Ken** and **Don**
Sports bags
Towels

Off stage: Squash racket (**Shaun**)
Squash racket (**Zoë**)

SCENE 2

Set: Small trees, fountain, seats, garden furniture, swing

Off stage: Small carrier bag. In it: pasties, crisps, bottle of wine, Mars bar (**Don**)
Bottle opener (**Don**)

Personal: **Shaun**: cigarette

SCENE 3

Strike: Small trees, fountain, seats, garden furniture, swing, all food and litter

Set: Sun lounger

Off stage: Squash racket (**Shaun**)
Large box containing sculpture (**Shirley**)

SCENE 4

Strike: Sun lounger

Off stage: Cassette player (**Zoë**)

SCENE 5

Strike: Cassette player

Off stage: Golf equipment (**Gertrude**)

LIGHTING PLOT

Practical fittings required: nil
Various interior and exterior settings

ACT I, SCENE 1

To open: Darkness

| Cue 1 | Disco music plays; when ready | (Page 1) |
| | *Bring up general interior lighting* | |

| Cue 2 | **Shirley** exits | (Page 6) |
| | *Change lights to different interior setting* | |

ACT I, SCENE 2

| Cue 3 | Music | (Page 11) |
| | *Fade lights* | |

ACT I, SCENE 3

To open: General interior lighting

| Cue 4 | Music | (Page 25) |
| | *Fade lights* | |

ACT I, SCENE 4

To open: General interior lighting

| Cue 5 | Music | (Page 32) |
| | *Fade lights* | |

ACT I, SCENE 5

To open: General interior lighting

| Cue 6 | **Chloë** massages **Don**'s forehead and temples | (Page 34) |
| | *Fade lights* | |

Lighting Plot

ACT I, SCENE 6

To open: Nightmare lighting

No cues

ACT II, SCENE 1

To open: Darkness

Cue 7   Noises of squash game   (Page 37)
           Snap up general interior lighting

Cue 8   Music   (Page 41)
           Black-out

ACT II, SCENE 2

To open: General exterior lighting; summer night effect

Cue 9   Music; **Don** slowly exits   (Page 54)
           Black-out

ACT II, SCENE 3

To open: General exterior lighting; morning effect

Cue 10   Music   (Page 61)
           Fade lights

ACT II, SCENE 4

To open: General interior lighting; evening effect

Cue 11   **Don**: " ... I was just getting into that!"   (Page 64)
           Black-out

ACT II, SCENE 5

To open: General exterior lighting; fresh morning effect

Cue 12   Music   (Page 69)
           Slowly fade lights

EFFECTS PLOT

ACT I

ACT II